Robin Lobban

THE FIRST WORLD WAR

Oxford University Press

Oxford University Press, Walton Street, Oxford OX2 6DP

Oxford New York Toronto
Delhi Bombay Calcutta Madras Karachi
Petaling Jaya Singapore Hong Kong Tokyo
Nairobi Dar es Salaam Cape Town
Melbourne Auckland

and associated companies in
Beirut Berlin Ibadan Nicosia

Oxford is a trade mark of Oxford University Press

ISBN 0 19 913283 6   © Oxford University Press 1982
                        First published 1982
                        Reprinted 1984, 1987, 1988

Phototypeset by Tradespools Limited, Frome, Somerset
Printed and bound in Great Britain by
William Clowes Limited, Beccles and London

CONTENTS

Chapter One

Europe in 1900

A European World

As the nineteenth century drew to a close, the peoples of Europe could perhaps look with confidence and some optimism towards the future and the twentieth century. The previous century had seen the European countries advance to new heights of political, scientific and economic power, and there seemed no reason why the great factories and industrial machines should not continue to pour out a flood of goods to increase the wealth and comforts of the peoples. Progress and advance seemed to be the keynote of this 'Mighty Continent', and the peoples and statesmen of the European countries could look around with pride and satisfaction as they compared their own lands with those of other regions of the world.

They had apparently every reason for such attitudes. From the fifteenth century European explorers, sailors, traders, missionaries and settlers had poured out to every continent, and now Europe in effect dominated the globe, even though it had only some 25 per cent of the world's population. Many of the European countries had huge empires in Africa, Asia, Australasia and the Americas, while large settlements of European peoples had taken place in every continent. Almost all of Africa had been divided up between the countries of Europe, while in Asia few territories outside China and Japan escaped their direct rule. In the Americas the United States and the Latin American republics in the south had secured their political independence, while the former British colony in Canada had become a Dominion with internal self government.

The United States of America was in a very special position and shared in Europe's general power and influence. The original thirteen colonies had won their independence from Britain at the end of the eighteenth century, and by 1900 the new nation had expanded across the continent to the Pacific and had become a great industrial giant. Formerly the Americans had been opposed to colonialism and had tried to keep themselves separate from the affairs of Europe, but in the few years

European emigrants to the United States, 1890

Europe in 1900

immediately before 1900 she had defeated the Spaniards in war and had herself seized an empire in the Caribbean and the Pacific. In so many ways the United States could properly be regarded as an extension of Europe, and indeed throughout the nineteenth century it had been the great goal of European migration. Between 1850 and 1900 almost seventeen million people crossed the Atlantic from Europe to make their homes there, and this movement was to continue in the early twentieth century with over eleven million European immigrants arriving in the United States between 1901 and 1910. The largest number in this latter period came from Italy with 3,615,000 and the United Kingdom (including Ireland) with 3,150,000.

Even those countries which lay outside the direct rule of Europe were penetrated by European influences, and everywhere European ideas in culture and technology were being copied and imitated. Europeans, too, controlled the world economy and trade, and the resources and raw materials of every continent were exploited for the advantage of Europe. The produce of the world, the cocoa, tea, sugar, rubber, nitrates, gold, wheat, cattle, sheep and other resources flowed to Europe to feed its industries and to satisfy the needs of its people. From Europe capital and investment streamed out to every corner of the world to earn rich returns for their owners. All this trade and investment was protected by the European navies which controlled the seas, and they could despatch powerful armies and forces to deal with any opposition or threat to their power and interests. In 1900, for instance, forces of nine nations were sent to China to crush the Boxer Rebellion when European lives and trade were threatened there.

In a sense all this pattern of European power and prestige was captured and symbolized by the great Paris World Fair of 1900. There was put on display all the glories, triumphs and achievements of France and of Europe, and great crowds came to see and admire the pavilions and exhibitions celebrating the wonders of industry, science and colonisation. There were colourful scenes of life in every continent in the world, but perhaps the most impressive and popular were the pavilions illustrating the recent advances in electricity, chemistry, engineering and aviation. A crowded centre of attraction was the magnificent Palace of Electricity which somehow seemed to sum up all the great European achievements of the past and to be a symbol of all their hopes and aspirations for the future:

'The Palace of Electricity glows nightly with dazzling lights, and there written, as it were, in letters of fire, will be found the history of electricity from its most primitive manifestations to its latest application: the telephone, bearer of winged words and herald of the television of the future which will transmit over long distances the living image of the person speaking. The fairy goddess of electricity has become a mighty sovereign, endowed, thanks to the genius of man, with infinite powers.'

France

The countries of Europe who exercised such influence in the world of 1900 varied greatly in size and power. Most prominent were the Great Powers of France, the German Empire, the Austro-Hungarian Empire, the Russian Empire, Italy and the

The Paris World Fair, 1900

The famous Moulin Rouge, Paris, 1900

6

United Kingdom. France was one of the oldest nations in Europe, and for centuries she had played a vital role in the affairs of the continent. Under Louis XIV in the seventeenth century and Napoleon in the early nineteenth century she had threatened to bring Europe under her control, but now perhaps she was overshadowed militarily and economically by Germany. Nevertheless, French prestige was still very high, and she possessed an extensive empire in Africa and Asia. From the Revolution of 1789 she had been regarded as the centre of a great revolutionary tradition, and her present government was a republican one. The cultural influence of France was world-wide, and indeed Paris was in a sense the leading centre of the theatre, art, fashion and high society. France was in the forefront of that restless European drive to conquer new fields and horizons, and thus she was a pioneer in developing the aeroplane. The sheer thrusting vigour and courage of the early airmen cannot perhaps be better illustrated than by the words spoken by the Frenchman, Captain Ferber, a short time before he was killed testing a new machine:

'To design a flying machine is nothing; to build one is nothing much; to try it in the air is everything.'

The German Empire

One of France's main rivals in the Europe of 1900 was the new and powerful Germany. Germany had been formed only in 1871 after France had been defeated in the Franco-Prussian war, for previously she had been a collection of states such as Prussia, Bavaria and Hanover. The new Germany had soon proved to be a potential giant, and by 1900 she was one of the strongest powers in Europe with a magnificent army and a growing navy. She had made great advances in industry, and now clearly

Prussian officers enjoying a meal

she was a leader in steel production and in the automobile and chemical industries. She had been late in entering the race for colonies, but she had managed to secure territories in Africa and the Pacific. German commerce was advancing at an astonishing rate, and German goods and merchants were challenging their rivals and competitors in almost every market in the world. Germany had a Parliament or Reichstag, but the main powers of government lay with the Emperor (Kaiser) and his ministers. The King of Prussia had become the Emperor of Germany in 1871, and now in 1900 the ruler was the Kaiser Wilhelm II. He was a restless, ambitious type of person, and his boasting and threatening statements, together with the growing strength of Germany, were increasingly sending shivers and alarm bells tingling in the capitals of all the other European states.

Italy

Another relatively new country was Italy which had been finally united in 1870. Previously Italy, too, had been divided into separate states, but after unification she had advanced to the ranks of the Great European Powers. She had acquired territories in Africa, and she had ambitions of exerting a dominating influence in the Mediterranean Sea. She had thriving new industries in northern Italy, but the south still remained poor and backward, and it was from this region that large numbers of immigrants were moving to the United States. Italy was a parliamentary monarchy, but although she was in effect one of the weaker members of the Great Powers, her rulers had ambitions of playing an influential role in European affairs.

The Austro-Hungarian Empire

Occupying a strategic and dominant position in Central Europe was the Austro-Hungarian Empire. The Austrian lands had been welded together over the centuries by their great ruling family, the Habsburgs, and by 1900 they controlled a multitude of peoples in Central and Eastern Europe including Germans, Magyars, Slavs, Czechs, Slovaks, Croats, Slovenes, Ruthenes, Poles, Italians and many others. The ruler was the Emperor Franz Josef who had come to the throne in 1848, and during his reign the Empire suffered painful reverses. In 1867 there had been formed the Dual Monarchy whereby the Empire was divided into an Austrian and a Hungarian part. Franz Josef was the ruler in both areas, but each had its own parliament, although foreign affairs and defence was still controlled by the Emperor. The Austrians or Germans were dominant in their area, while the Magyars were dominant in Hungary, and each ruled over the other peoples within their territory. Earlier in 1859 Austrian territories had been lost in Italy, while in 1866 Austria had lost influence in Germany when she was defeated by Prussia. Now increasingly the Slav peoples of the Empire were demanding more freedom and independence, and this presented great problems for the Emperor and further threatened his power.

Russian troops on parade in the Imperial Indoor Riding School

The Russian Empire

Another great and multi-racial Empire at this time was the Russian Empire. Russia had spread out over the centuries from a small principality round Moscow, and by 1900 it was a colossus stretching from Poland and the Baltic right across Europe and Asia to the Pacific and ruling over many European and Asiatic peoples. Over the years Russian armies had played a vital role in European struggles, and the other countries feared the huge potential strength of the 'Great Russian Bear'. She was ruled by an autocratic Czar, Nicholas II ('Czar', 'Kaiser' and the Latin word 'Caesar' have the same origin), but by 1900 his power was being somewhat weakened by the growth of revolutionary movements within the Russian territories.

Britain

The sixth of the European Great Powers was Britain (see Chapter 2). Britain had been the first country to become industrialised and for much of the nineteenth century she had been the leading industrial power. She had built up a massive empire with territories and colonies in every continent, and she had the world's most powerful navy. Her form of government was that of a parliamentary democracy, and she tended to favour movements for democracy and national freedom in other countries.

The smaller powers

Outside the ranks of the Great Powers were a number of other countries that made up the European scene in 1900. In the north were the Baltic countries of Denmark and Sweden, although here Norway was to separate from Sweden in 1905. On the Iberian peninsula were Spain and Portugal, both of whom had formerly played a great part in the affairs of Europe and in the story of European colonisation. In the strategic border areas between France and Germany were the small powers of Luxembourg, Belgium and Holland. Both Belgium and Holland were advanced industrial and commercial powers, but they were weaker militarily and feared attacks from the neighbouring Great Powers. Further east was the prosperous, mountainous and neutral Switzerland, while in the Balkans were Greece, Romania, Bulgaria and Serbia, a group of rather less economically advanced states that had been formed out of the Turkish Empire a few years earlier. Their former ruler, the Turkish Empire, had once controlled much of Central and Eastern Europe, but although it still retained a large empire in Western Asia, its power in Europe had declined and it had lost territories to Russia and to these new Balkan states. In their remaining European territories the subject peoples were increasingly eager to secure independence, while the Balkan countries were determined to advance their frontiers at Turkey's expense.

The ruling families of Europe

Although there was a wide variety of countries and communities in Europe in 1900, there were many ties and links that drew them together into a common European society. Thus although there were widely differing types of government which included the republic of France, the parliamentary democracy of Britain, the Empires of Germany and Austro-Hungary, and the Czarist autocracy of Russia, yet the rulers of Europe retained close ties with each other. Apart from the republics of France and Switzerland, all countries had a ruling royal family, and these were in most instances closely related by family or marriage bonds. Queen Victoria of Britain, for example, was related to almost all the royal families of Europe, and at frequent intervals she held great family gatherings attended by many of the rulers on the Continent:

> 'Queen Victoria's descendants filled the thrones of Europe; they carried the distinguished tradition of Victoria to the Empires of Germany and Russia, to the Kingdoms of Greece and Romania and later to those of Norway and Spain: as well as to countless duchies and dynasties in the heart of Germany. As we turn to those great family gatherings which she loved, and look perhaps on the picture of the Queen and her descendants and see the gay uniforms and the long shrewd Coburg faces we become conscious of an international force which was powerful so long as the central figure lived to keep it together.'

One frequent visitor to Queen Victoria and Britain was her grandson, the German Kaiser Wilhelm II, and during the 1890s he came regularly to the Isle of Wight for Cowes week:

Queen Victoria with some of her family. (Can you find Kaiser Wilhelm, Tsar Nicholas and the Prince of Wales?)

'The Emperor's arrival was always impressive. When the imperial yacht *Hohenzollern* entered the harbour escorted by a group of German warships, the Royal Navy gave it a twenty-one gun salute and the hundreds of private craft lying in anchor dipped their pennants. From then on there was an elaborate round of festivities; the Queen gave a state banquet at Osborne, the Prince of Wales entertained nightly at the Royal Yacht Club, German and British bands vied with each other to serenade the townspeople, the two navies exchanged a flow of hospitality and hostesses fought with each other to fill the gaps.'

The nobles, aristocracy and upper classes of Europe, too, had many common ties and interests. Some families were linked by marriage, while the social life of the Continent frequently brought nobles from many countries together. There would

Kaiser Wilhelm in a kilt

express even ran from St. Petersburg through Vienna to Cannes to bring the Russian Princes and Grand Dukes and the Austrian Counts to the Mediterranean. Biarritz was a truly international resort with aristocrats from many countries apparently quite willing to look on as the British ruling classes took their own sports abroad with them:

'In perfect weather the Biarritz and Bayonne Foxhounds met on Saturday in the grounds of the Hotel d'Angleterre. Among the spectators and others looking on in automobiles and carriages were the Grand Duke Alexander and his family, Prince Alexander of Oldenburg, Princess Eugenie of Oldenburg, the Duke of Leuchtenbourg, Sir Malcolm and Lady Morris, Mrs Cavendish-Bentinck, Mrs J. Tyrwhitt Drake.'

The ruling class at play. Henley-on-Thames

be great international parties in a German or French castle, while there was a regular cosmopolitan season which saw the upper classes visiting different parts of Europe throughout the year. After spending June and July in London, the fashionable world would visit the German spas until September, and then they would move on to various country houses or castles till December. From December till May many frequented the resorts of Monte Carlo or Biarritz. A special international

Culture and religion

Culture and religion, too, had an international aspect at this time. The theatre, music, opera and art moved freely across the frontiers of Europe, while the works of the great musicians and dramatists of Europe were known and performed in all countries. Great theatre companies and orchestras toured all the major cities, and some companies had an international cast. Thus, for example, the Vienna State Opera in 1900 drew in the world's most famous singers, conductors and composers, and the performances at the famous Concert Hall were often truly European occasions. Religion was another unifying bond, for although there were different creeds in Protestantism, Roman Catholicism and Greek Orthodox Christianity, yet the Christian religion pervaded the whole life of the Continent. The local church was the focal point for many communities in every land, and everywhere the sound of church bells was a reminder of the common heritage of Christendom.

Economics

There were also many common features in the economic and social life of the Continent in 1900. The Industrial Revolution which began in Britain at the end of the eighteenth century had affected most of the countries of Western Europe, and over the years the wealth and produce of the Continent had expanded greatly. For much of the nineteenth century the textile industries and the heavy industries of steel, shipbuilding, engineering and mining had been the growth points of industrial advance, but in the final decades of the century the chemical and electrical industries had experienced radical changes. There had also been vital developments in transport with the construction of a railway network throughout the Continent, and more recently

Inside the Krupps munitions factory. Germany, 1910

in the years immediately before 1900 with the appearance of the diesel engine, the motor car and the aeroplane.

Europe had also developed a sophisticated financial system by 1900. Each of the Great Powers had different currencies, but they were linked together by a complex system of values based on gold. Throughout the Continent, too, there was a network of stock exchanges where finance was raised and investments in the great European companies was organized. Some of the great financiers were truly international in their operations, and none more so perhaps than the famous Rothschilds. By 1900 there were five brothers active in finance, with one being stationed in each of the following cities: London, Paris, Vienna, Frankfurt and Naples. They and others like them moved their money and capital from one country to another to take advantage of the opportunities that might present themselves in any area.

The great economic changes had also produced similar social developments throughout the Continent. Thus while the majority of people still lived and worked on the land as peasants, there were everywhere great and crowded towns and cities where the new industrial workers lived close to their mills and factories. Many of them lived in grim conditions in slums and overcrowded houses, and often the health standards were extremely low. An increasingly powerful and influential class of wealthy merchants, industrialists, lawyers, doctors etc. had also appeared in many European cities, and these lived a much more comfortable life in their fine town or country houses.

Socialism

The serious hardships and evils produced by the Industrial Revolution had inspired the growth of socialist movements in many European countries, and these movements with their stress on public ownership and social reforms sometimes had an international aspect. A First International Working-men's Association had been founded in 1864; and a Second International in 1889, and these helped to forge links between the socialists of all countries. Many believed that these ties and the actions that could be taken by workers would help

French foundry workers

prevent the outbreak of war in Europe. The workers would refuse to join in a struggle against their fellow-workers in other countries, and thus the plans of the military leaders would be foiled.

Rivalries: nationalism

And yet despite all these factors that tended to link together the countries and peoples of Europe, there were strong and traditional rivalries that emphasised their separate and individual identities. For centuries the European Powers had engaged in bitter struggles and wars, and in the nineteenth century the old disputes were intensified as the forces of nationalism swept through the Continent and as each people or nation sought to secure and advance its own position. Where a nation had been recently formed as with Germany or Italy, they sought to enhance their power and prestige, but where a people remained subject to another, then they plotted to gain their freedom and existence as a nation. In 1900 men could look back on a period of peace since the Franco-Prussian War of 1870, but there was a whole range of rivalries and tensions that wracked the Continent and kept the various countries at loggerheads.

Rivalries: France and Germany

One of the great rivalries of Europe was that which existed between the French and the Germans. For centuries France had sought to keep Germany weak and divided, but the Prussian victory in 1870 had altered the balance by creating a united Germany. The victorious Germans had seized the provinces of Alsace and Lorraine and had incorporated them into the German Empire, and this loss was bitterly resented by the French. The statues of the provinces in Paris were kept draped to illustrate the

Prussian officers outside the Palace of Versailles, 1871

these new countries were themselves fierce rivals and potential enemies, and they watched each other's every action with anxiety and suspicion. This situation was made even more dangerous by the rivalries and ambitions of the Great Powers in that region. Russia had long desired to extend her control to Constantinople, and this brought her into conflict with Austria who wished to drive eastwards into the Balkans and to bring the area under her influence. Any Austrian advance, moreover, was barred by the small state of Serbia, and the ensuing hostility between Serbia and Austria was intensified by the fact that the Serbians were issuing propaganda designed to take the southern Slav peoples away from the Austrian Empire. Russia saw herself as the protector of the Serbians and the other Slav peoples in the Balkans, and this also increased her rivalry with Austria. A number of the Balkan peoples were also Orthodox Christians like the Russians, and this gave them a further pretext for intervention. In the years up to 1900, too, Germany

French mourning at their loss, and continually the French leaders and people longed for the day when they could gain their revenge and recover them. The loss was all the more grievous because of the fact that the booming iron fields of Lorraine were now being used to make the German economy even more prosperous. Alsace-Lorraine seemed to symbolize the old, traditional Franco-German rivalry, and it appeared to many observers that the seeds of a future war might there be taking root.

Rivalries: the Balkans

Another area of tension and danger in Europe was the Balkans with its mixture of peoples and its centuries-old rivalries and enmities. The decline of Turkish power had given the Bulgarians, Romanians, Serbians and Greeks the opportunity to win their independence, and now they wished to free the remaining territories from Turkish control. But

Galata Bridge, Constantinople

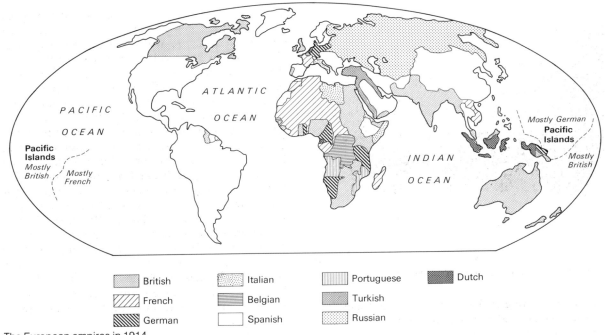

British		Italian		Portuguese		Dutch	
French		Belgian		Turkish			
German		Spanish		Russian			

The European empires in 1914

became increasingly interested in the area, and her drive eastwards brought her into conflict with Russian interests.

Rivalries: commerce and colonies

Another significant source of tension in the Europe of 1900 sprang from colonial and commercial rivalry between the Powers. As Europe became more industrialised, the various countries struggled to secure supplies of raw materials for their industries and markets for their goods. There were fierce disputes, too, as the European Powers sought to gain control over the last surviving colonial areas, and thus the rush to carve up Africa in the 1880s had created new and dangerous rivalries.

Alliances

The tensions created by these various quarrels and disputes were intensified and brought together by a series of alliances that had arisen over the previous two decades. These had been initiated by Bismarck, the German Chancellor, who had feared that the French desire for revenge after 1871 might lead her to seek an ally against Germany. He had drawn together Russia, Austria and Germany in a League of the Three Emperors in the 1870s and so kept France isolated, but then when Russian and Austrian rivalries in the Balkans forced him to choose, he had formed a Dual Alliance between Austria and Germany in 1879. This bound the two countries to give each other military support against a Russian attack:

'Should one of the two Empires be attacked by Russia, the high contracting parties bind themselves to come to the assistance of each other with the whole military strength of their Empire.

Should one of the high contracting parties be attacked by another power, the other party binds itself to observe at least a benevolent neutral attitude towards its fellow contracting party.

Should the attacking party in such a case be supported by Russia, the obligation of reciprocal assistance with the whole fighting force which is stipulated in Article 1 of this treaty becomes equally operative.'

In 1882 Italy joined this alliance to make it the Triple Alliance, with each power guaranteeing the other's full military support if either one were attacked by two other states. Later Bismarck managed to restore some agreement with Russia in the Reinsurance Treaty of 1887, but when he was forced by the Kaiser to resign in 1890, Germany no longer made any real attempt to keep Russia linked to her. Russia, now fearful of the German-Austrian friendship, moved closer to France, and in 1894 a military alliance was signed between these two countries:

'France and Russia, being animated by no other object than to meet the necessities of a defensive war, provoked by an attack of the forces of the Triple Alliance against one or other of them, have agreed upon the following provisions:

If France is attacked by Germany, or by Italy supported by Germany, Russia shall employ all her available forces to attack Germany.

If Russia is attacked by Germany, or by Austria supported by Germany, France shall employ all her available forces to fight Germany.'

DROPPING THE PILOT.

The Kaiser sacked Bismarck in 1890

The crossroads

With the creation of this Dual Alliance between Russia and France, Europe had been divided into two armed camps. Over the years to 1900 both sides steadily built up their armies and armaments, and over the Continent men could see gathering the dark and threatening storm clouds of international quarrels and disputes. But the age was also one of bright hope and optimism, and many people in 1900 were confident that they would soon witness further advances in science, industry and civilisation that would equal and even surpass any that had gone before. Thus when the new century dawned on 1 January 1901, Europe in a sense stood at a vital crossroads in its history when the future could go either way – either towards new triumphs and prosperity, or into a dark and bitter struggle that could threaten the whole fabric of Europe and European society. In the following chapters we shall trace the fortunes of the 'Mighty Continent' and the path that was followed in those early years of the twentieth century.

Bleriot, after his historic Channel crossing

Exercises   Chapter One

1 a) Describe those forces and trends in Europe in 1900 that helped bring the various countries together into a common European society.   7
  b) Outline the main problems that produced rivalry and tension in Europe in 1900.   7
  c) Which of these opposing forces, the factors bringing the countries together or those making them rivals, might seem the stronger to a person living in 1900?   6
                                                        (20)

2 The following is an extract from the Dual Alliance between France and Russia, 1894.
'France and Russia, being animated by no other object that to meet the necessities of a defensive war, provoked by an attack of the forces of the Triple Alliance against one or other of them, have agreed upon the following provisions:
'If France is attacked by Germany, or by Italy supported by Germany, Russia shall employ all her available forces to attack Germany.
'If Russia is attacked by Germany, or by Austria supported by Germany, France shall employ all her available forces to fight Germany.'

  a) According to the extract, which country was regarded as the greatest threat by Russia and France?   2
  b) Explain how and why the powers of the Triple Alliance had come together in their alliance. 6
  c) What were the main reasons why Russia and France agreed to form this alliance?   5
  d) Would you agree that the aims of Russia and France were entirely defensive?   2
  e) How did the formation of this Dual Alliance between Russia and France affect the general diplomatic situation in Europe?   5
                                                        (20)

3 Imagine you have paid a visit to the Paris World Fair in 1900. Write a letter home to a friend telling of your experiences and your thoughts about the significance of the Exhibition for European achievements and Europe's position in the world.   (20)

Chapter Two

Britain 1900–14

Britain in 1900

Of all the European Powers, Britain was perhaps the most representative of that world dominion and control which the Continent exercised in 1900. By 1900 she had built up the largest empire of all the European countries, with territories, colonies and dominions in every corner of the globe. Some colonies like Canada, Australia and New Zealand had become self-governing dominions within the British Empire, but they still retained the closest of ties with the Mother Country. To protect this great empire and her imperial communications, Britain had the world's most powerful navy. She also had a small regular army which was normally used in small border skirmishes in the Empire, but in 1900 it was engaged in a more serious struggle against the Boer republics of the Transvaal and the Orange Free State in South Africa (Boer War, 1899–1902). The Boers (descendants of Dutch settlers in Africa) initially inflicted serious defeats on the British Army, and it was not until 1902 that Britain managed to overcome them and force them to make peace. The Boer republics were taken over, but later they were joined with Cape Colony and Natal to form the Union of South Africa as another Dominion within the Empire.

The British economy

In the pattern of her economy, too, Britain represented well that industrial and scientific supremacy that had advanced Europe to the foremost position in the world in 1900. She had been the first country in the world to experience an Industrial Revolution at the end of the eighteenth century, and by the middle of the nineteenth century she had become the 'Workshop of the World' sending manufactured goods to all parts of the world in return for her large imports of foodstuffs and raw materials. Her increasing wealth and capital was often directed outwards to overseas enterprises, and these foreign investments brought rich returns and helped maintain Britain's strong financial position in the world. Towards the end of the nineteenth century British farming experienced a serious depression as her policy of Free Trade allowed in cheaper foreign products, but in 1900 her principal industries of shipbuilding, engineering, mining and

Wounded British soldiers during the Boer War

The British Empire in 1914

steel were still flourishing. Her former dominant position was being strongly challenged, however, as the United States and Germany began forging ahead in the production of steel and other basic commodities. Germany, too, was prominent in new fields like the chemical, electrical and automobile industries, while her goods were flooding into traditional British markets and even into Britain itself. Britain was still an immensely strong economic unit in 1900, but the days of unrivalled success in world markets were now over.

British society

The successes of British industry and the British economy had brought great wealth into the coun-try, but that wealth had not been distributed equally among all sections of the population. On the one hand, it brought great benefits to the old ruling classes and to the new middle classes of industrialists, merchants, bankers, lawyers, doctors etc. Increased rents and revenues came to the rich upper classes, and by the early twentieth century many of them were leading luxurious and leisured lives:

'I used to take my sons riding with me in Windsor Great Park every morning,' wrote one titled lady. 'In the afternoons we used often to watch polo, also in the park. We also played games – lawn tennis and croquet, and especially golf. We always had a large house party for Ascot

Races, and all our friends had people staying with them too, and there were dinner parties and balls every night during race week. These full days of gaiety involved rapid changes of dress. We wore chiffon and lace dresses at Ascot with large, becoming picture hats. We would rush home from the racecourse and change quickly into linen or cotton dresses in order to go to the river, enjoying late afternoon sunlight on the cushions of the punts until it was time to change for dinner. The Life Guards used to give a ball in their barracks during Ascot Week, and there were many other excellent dances.'

For the wealthy middle classes, too, life seemed good at this time. They lived in substantial town or country houses, with large numbers of servants to cater for their every need. Like their upper class neighbours, they followed a busy social life of hunting, dinner parties, balls and visits to the theatre or opera. They were very concerned about maintaining their social prestige and position, and many of them consulted the etiquette books written at this time:

The ball: 'At a ball given in town a hostess should receive her guests at the head of the staircase, and at the door of the ball-room at a country-house ball. She should shake hands with each guest in the order of their arrival. A lady and gentleman should not ascend the staircase or make their entrance into the ball-room arm in arm. A ball is usually opened either by the hostess herself or by one of her daughters. Opening a ball simply signifies dancing the first quadrille at the top of the room with a gentleman of the highest rank present.'

The theatre: 'It is a piece of bad manners to enter the theatre late, and it is equally rude to leave before the entertainment is ended, unless the interval be chosen when nothing is going on.

In the ballroom

Refreshments are frequently carried round by attendants to private boxes, and sometimes in the stalls as well. Should they appear, it is the duty of the gentleman of the party to ask the ladies if they wish for any, and to pay for what is consumed. It is, however, a rare thing for ladies to eat or drink at the play. The gentleman also pays for the programme at the few theatres where a charge is made.'

The chaperon: 'No sooner has a young lady left the schoolroom and dispensed with the chaperonage of the governess, than she requires the chaperonage of a married lady. At country out-door gatherings, the chaperonage is of comparatively slight nature, but at all other entertainments it is imperative that a young lady should be accompanied by a chaperon; and a young lady who attempts to evade this received rule would be considered unconventional. A good chaperon will introduce the young lady under her care to those ladies of her acquaintance who are most in the habit of giving entertainments, and will introduce any gentleman to her whom she thinks would be likely to ask her to dance.'

Contrasts in wealth and poverty, leisure and labour

By contrast, many of the ordinary people and workers living in the towns and rural districts of Britain in 1900 were experiencing considerable poverty and hardships. The conditions in London were investigated by Charles Booth, a London shipowner, and in a report published in 1902 he calculated that about 35 per cent of the capital's population were living in poverty and want. He painted a terrible picture of suffering, crime and drunkenness among the casual workers and unemployed, and his vivid accounts had a powerful effect on his readers:

'Along Crescent Street (in Hammersmith), the beerhouse at the corner full; more women than men inside; hatless women, with white aprons, rough hair and bare arms, and with shawls round their shoulders. Many women in the beerhouses at either end of Bangor Street. Men here were coming home full, sullen, solitary, addressed by no one and speaking to no one. In St. Anne's Road three young women of laundry type, singing, arm-in-arm, reeling, noisily drunk; one with a small baby in her arms. Then into Norland Road, another woman drunk and noisy and a few men equally drunk; one woman in a drunken torpor, sitting on the pavement propped against the wall.'

The housing conditions for many people were quite appalling, even although some improvements had been carried out in the later nineteenth century. Here, for example, is the picture painted of a group of miners' houses in Scotland:

'The Miners' Row is often a dreary place, with houses arranged in monotonous lines or squares. The older house is either a "single-end" or "but-and-ben", according as it has one or two rooms. It has only one door, and the solid back wall is pierced only by the smallest of windows, if by any, so that through ventilation does not exist.

'Occasionally there is a properly constructed common washhouse, but in the older villages more often only such makeshift and ramshackle washhouses and coalsheds as the miners have run up for themselves. But the chief of these unsightly structures are the privies. These are large erections, open on one side, where ashes and all other household refuse are thrown in, and closed on the side which serves as latrine. It is the only sanitary convenience in many rows; and it is so foul-smelling, and so littered with filth of all sort, that no decent woman can use it, while if the children do so, it is at grave risk to their health of body and mind.'

Not surprisingly the people living in such conditions often suffered from serious illnesses and disease. Earlier in the nineteenth century the situation had been even worse when the population had been ravaged by attacks of cholera, typhus and other fevers, but even although the Public Health Movement had helped provide clean water and better sanitation in most places, the health record of Britain was still quite unsatisfactory in 1900. The Boer War, for example, revealed the extent of the damage done by generations of industrialisation when some 40 per cent of the men medically examined were found to be unfit for military service, with the figures in Manchester and other black spots reaching 66 per cent. The infant mortality rates also told a grim tale, with 145 children in every 1000 dying before reaching the age of one.

The government of Britain

Responsibility for dealing with these and other problems lay with the British Parliament and Government. Britain still had a monarch, Queen Victoria, on the throne, but over the years the monarch's powers had been steadily reduced until by 1900 the real authority lay with the two Houses of Parliament, the Lords and the Commons. The Prime Minister and other Ministers were members of the party having a majority in the House of Commons, and they remained in office as long as they retained the support of Parliament or until a new election. Elections were held at least every seven years, and by 1900 nearly every man in the country had a vote. Women were still excluded from the franchise, but there was a growing demand that they, too, should be given the vote.

The two main political parties at this time were the Conservatives and the Liberals. The Conservatives were perhaps the party of the Empire, the Church and tradition, while the Liberals stressed Free Trade, reform and individual freedom. In 1900 the Conservatives were in office, and in that year they won a substantial majority at an election where enthusiasm for the Boer War favoured their imperial policies. 1900, too, saw the appearance of a new British political party with the formation of the Labour Representation Committee by representatives of several socialist societies and the trade unions. The Labour Representation Committee sought to return M.P.s who would represent directly the interests of labour and the workers, and in 1906 it was transformed into the Labour Party. It won 53 seats in the election of 1906, and with its growing influence it threatened to break the old mould of British politics.

Why was Lloyd George given the credit for the Liberal reforms?

THE PHILANTHROPIC HIGHWAYMAN.

Mr. Lloyd-George. "I'LL MAKE 'EM PITY THE AGED POOR!"

The Liberal reforms

The 1906 election also witnessed a landslide victory for the Liberals after the Conservative Government had resigned at the end of 1905. The Liberals were led by Sir Henry Campbell-Bannerman and later by Herbert Asquith, and they included in their ranks some very able politicians like David Lloyd George and Winston Churchill. They now began concentrating on the grim social conditions that existed in Britain, for they, like so many people in Britain, had been shocked by the reports of ill-health and deprivation presented by Booth and others. Already in the 1880s Germany had introduced state insurance schemes to deal with the problems of poverty and unemployment, and now these could be studied to see if they could be used in Britain. There was also a general feeling in Britain that she must take steps to improve her health record so that her military strength would not be fatally impaired.

The first problem to be tackled was that of the children who too often were the first casualties of an industrial society. In 1906 free school meals were introduced for the children of very poor families, while in the following year an act was passed providing for the medical inspection of children in schools. In 1908 measures were brought in aimed at preventing the ill-treatment of children, while special juvenile courts were set up to try children who had broken the law. By these provisions it was hoped that any illnesses or diseases would be detected at an early age, and that any children forced into crime would receive treatment appropriate to their age and situation.

Further welfare measures soon followed for other needy sections of the community. In 1908 non-contributory old age pensions were introduced, with 5 shillings (25p) per week being given to single persons over 70, 7 shillings 6 pence

(37½p) to married couples with an income of less than £26 per year. This measure was a great boon to the old and kept many of them out of the workhouses when they were too old to secure employment. In 1909 Labour Exchanges were set up to help the unemployed find work, and then in 1911 came the vitally important National Insurance Act. This was in two parts, Part I dealing with sickness and ill health, and Part II with unemployment. Part I set up an insurance fund to provide benefits for workers earning less than £160 a year. Affected workers paid 4 pence (2p) a week into the fund, their employers paid 3 pence (1½p) and the state 2 pence (1p). The money was used to provide medical attention for the insured workers, to pay them sickness benefits for a period up to 26 weeks, and to provide a maternity benefit of 30 shillings (£1.50) for their wives. Part II covered workers in industries like building, construction and shipbuilding who suffered periods of unemployment, and provided for an unemployment payment of 15 shillings (75p) a week for up to 15 weeks in any one year.

Although there were still many social evils to be dealt with in Britain, the welfare measures of the Liberals were indeed a great step forward. Lloyd George, the Chancellor of the Exchequer, in a colourful speech, spoke of the good that they would do for the weaker sections of the community:

'I can see another vision. I can see the Old Age Pension Act, the National Insurance Act, and many another Act in their trail descending, like breezes from the hills of my native land (Wales), sweeping into the mist-laden valleys, and clearing the gloom away until the rays of God's sun have pierced the narrowest window.'

But the wealthy and propertied classes were not nearly so enthusiastic, and they mounted a fierce

Collecting the first old age pension, 1909

campaign against some of the measures. The newspapers, for example, spoke feelingly of the indignity suffered by mistresses forced by the National Insurance Act to 'lick stamps' to put on the cards of their domestic servants. They had been even more enraged in 1909 when to pay for the reforms Lloyd George had, in his 'People's Budget', raised income tax, introduced a supertax on incomes over £5,000 a year, increased death duties, imposed taxes on motor cars, petrol, tobacco and alcohol, and taxed the 'unearned increment' or rise in land value when a piece of land was sold or inherited. The daughter of the Duke of Rutland recorded the grim effect on her father: 'We all thought Papa would die. He looked too ashen to recover.' Lloyd George was not dismayed, however, and retaliated by attacking the selfishness of his rich opponents:

'Who ordained that a few should have the

land of Britain? Who made ten thousand people owners of the soil, and the rest of us trespassers in the land of our birth? Who is it who is responsible for the scheme of things whereby one man is engaged through life in grinding labour to win a bare and precarious subsistence for himself, and when, at the end of his days, he claims at the hands of the community he served a poor pension of 8 pence (3½p) a day, he can get it only through a revolution; and another man who does not toil receives every hour of the day, every hour of the night, whilst he slumbers, more than his poor neighbour receives in a whole year of toil?'

House of Lords

So great was the opposition aroused by Lloyd George's taxation proposals that the House of Lords refused to pass the People's Budget. The Liberal Governments had frequently been obstructed by the Lords in the past, and now they decided to introduce a Parliament Act to cut down their powers. In 1910 two elections were held over this issue, and on each occasion the Liberals were returned to office. In 1910 the Budget was at last passed by the Lords, but the Liberals continued with their proposals to reform Parliament. At length when the King agreed that he would create a sufficient number of new peers to pass the Bill, the Lords gave way and the Parliament Act of 1911 was passed. It stated that the House of Lords could not touch a finance Bill, while for other measures any Bill that was passed in three successive sessions in the Commons would become law despite the Lords' opposition. The length of a Parliament was reduced from seven years to five, while another measure provided for the payment of M.P.s. A great step forward had been taken in securing the supremacy of the House of Commons, and the British Parlia-mentary system became that much more democratic.

The suffragettes

The Liberal Government was faced with certain other problems in these years before 1914, notably that presented by the growth of the suffragette movement demanding that women should be given the right to vote. Women held a sadly under-privileged position in British society at the end of the nineteenth century, but early in the twentieth century small groups of middle class women began demanding the vote. In 1903 a group known as the suffragettes was formed under the leadership of Mrs Emmeline Pankhurst and her two daughters, Christabel and Sylvia, and they began holding great rallies and demonstrations. When the Government failed to respond, they turned to violence, chaining themselves to railings, setting fire to pillar boxes, interrupting meetings and setting fire to houses and clubs. The authorities arrested the law-breakers, and when the suffragettes went on hunger strike, they introduced the cruel practice of forced feeding. Next the Government brought in the 'Cat and Mouse Act' whereby suffragettes could be released from prison and then rearrested after they had recovered. A sad incident occurred when one suffragette was killed throwing herself in front of the King's horse at the Derby; and tension mounted as the two sides, the Government and the suffragettes, remained as obstinate and determined as ever.

Ireland

Another difficult and complex problem in the years before the First World War was that of Ireland. Ireland had long been under British control, and in 1800 by the terms of the Act of Union she had been united with Britain. Throughout the nineteenth

Suffragettes under arrest after an attack on Buckingham Palace, 1914

century religious and land reforms were introduced in an attempt to remove the grievances of the Irish, but many of them remained utterly opposed to the connection with Britain. A Home Rule League was founded in 1872, and this led the Liberals to introduce Home Rule Bills in 1886 and 1893. Both were defeated, however, the first in the House of Commons, and the second in the House of Lords.

The Liberal Government elected in 1906 turned once more to deal with the Irish question, and in 1912 it introduced a third Home Rule Bill into Parliament. The Lords rejected it, but under the provisions of the 1911 Parliament Act it would become law in 1914. But there was considerable opposition to the proposals in Ulster, the mainly Protestant area in north-east Ireland. An organization known as the Ulster Volunteers was formed to resist Home Rule, and they were soon engaged in drillings and gun runnings. Nationalists also began preparing for a struggle, and the situation became quite critical. Further difficulties arose for the Government when a group of army officers stationed at the Curragh in Ireland declared in 1914 that they were not prepared to march against Ulster to put down any resistance to the Home Rule Act. In Britain the Conservatives increased the tension

A procession of Ulster Volunteers. Portadown, 1912

by supporting the Ulstermen, and thus by 1914 there was a real prospect that civil war might break out in Ireland, and that such a struggle would bitterly divide the British people.

Trade unions

Another area of conflict in the pre-war years existed in the field of labour and industrial relations. The trade union movement had been growing in strength during the second half of the nineteenth century, and by 1900 it was a powerful force in the land. It suffered reverses in the law courts early in the twentieth century, but the Liberal Government restored its powers by passing a Trade Disputes Act in 1906 stating that unions could not be sued for damages caused by the actions of their members during a strike, and a Trade Union Act in 1913 giving them the right to impose levies on their members to be used to support the Labour Party or for other political purposes. Industrial unrest continued to grow, however, and between 1910 and 1914 a great series of strikes was launched. These caused serious disruptions in the national life, and many were accompanied by violence. During a strike of railwaymen and dockers in Liverpool in 1911, for example, the city was almost in a state of siege for a month as strikers fought troops and policemen, and on one occasion a huge crowd marched to the town hall and set it on fire. The industrial struggles were intensified in 1914 when a Triple Alliance of miners, railwaymen and transport workers was formed to cooperate in all future disputes. Steadily a growing element of bitterness and class conflict was entering the scene:

'The working class and the employing class have nothing in common. There can be no peace so long as hunger and want are found among millions of working people, and the few, who make up the employing class, have all the good

Troops and police sent into Liverpool to quell strike disturbances, 1911

things in life. These conditions can be changed and the interest of the working class upheld only by an organisation formed in such a way that all its members in any one industry, or in all industries if necessary, cease work whenever a strike or lock-out is on in any department, thus making an injury to one an injury to all.'

Social life

All these growing difficulties and tensions in Britain, however, must be set against a background of vigorous and exciting developments in the general life of the community. Though many of the people were still poor, there was undoubtedly a lively social life, and many varied entertainments were available in the towns and cities of Britain. The old music hall was a wonderful centre of amusement and entertainment, and it attracted large audiences to see the singers, dancers, comedians, acrobats and other artists. Also appearing were the new cinema palaces where wonder-struck audiences could see the miracle of the movie film. Spectator sports had also developed towards the end of the nineteenth century, and large crowds attended association football or first class cricket games. Reports of these activities were given in the popular, mass circulation newspapers that were appearing in this period, among them the *Daily Mail* in 1896, the *Daily Express* in 1900, the *Daily Mirror* in 1903, the *Daily Sketch* in 1909, the *Daily Herald* in 1911. People also benefited from the railway network laid down in the 1840s and 1850s, and many of them took advantage of the cheap fares to visit the seaside resorts for annual holidays or for day trips. A real transport revolution was also taking place in the early years of the twentieth century with the appearance of the motor-car and the motor-bus. The early motor-cars were sold principally to the rich and wealthy, but the motor-omnibus made speedier transport available to people in both town and country. The extent to which the internal combustion engine was to transform the lives of the people can perhaps be seen in the virtual disappearance of the horse from the towns and cities. In 1900 there were some 36,000 horses pulling tramcars in British towns and cities, but by 1914 this number had dwindled to 900.

Leisure activities. The Music Hall (left) and the seaside (above). Meanwhile, popular newspapers flourished. Inside the *Daily Mail* office (top).

Britain and Europe

The early years of the twentieth century, therefore, witnessed considerable changes and developments in Britain. People were thrilled at the progress being made, and, like everyone in Europe at the time, they looked forward with some optimism to further developments, discoveries and inventions. But at the same time there was a growing fear that the security they had known for so long was being threatened by all the struggles at home and by gathering clouds on the international scene. Thus Britain, too, stood at the crossroads in the early years of the twentieth century, with the prospect of peace and progress, on the one side, and a danger of conflict and war, on the other. In the next chapter we shall trace the mounting crises and the response of the British statesmen and people to the great challenge that lay before them.

An early motor-car

Exercises   Chapter Two

1 a) Explain how each of the following presented problems for the Liberal Government in Britain in the years before 1914:
   i) The House of Lords
   ii) The Suffragettes
   iii) Ireland
   iv) The Trade Unions   *8*

b) With what success did the Liberal Government tackle each of these problems?   *8*
c) 'The Years of Strife.' How apt a title is this for the years 1910–14 in British domestic history?   *4*
                                                        (20)

2 The following is an extract from a speech made by Lloyd George in 1908.
'I do not think the better-off classes, whose comfort is assured, realise the sufferings of the unemployed workmen. What is poverty? Have you felt it yourselves? If not, you ought to thank God for having been spared its sufferings and its temptations. Have you seen others enduring it? Then pray God to forgive you, if you have not done your best to alleviate it.'

a) What measures did Lloyd George and the Liberal Governments (1905–14) introduce to help the unemployed in Britain?   *4*
b) What other measures did they bring in to help the poor, the sick, the young and the aged?   *6*
c) Explain why the Liberal Governments were ready and prepared to introduce such reforms.   *3*
d) Which groups in Britain opposed these reforms and what were the reasons for their opposition?   *3*
e) To what extent did these social reforms transform Britain into a 'Welfare State'?   *4*
                                                        (20)

3 'The Good Old Days.' Imagine you are living in Britain in 1920, and under the above title write an article for a magazine describing life in Britain before 1914 and discussing what it was really like.   *(20)*

Chapter Three

The approach to war

The rival alliances

Up until about 1900 Britain remained aloof from the rival alliances that, as we saw in Chapter 1, arranged the European Powers into competing blocs. She had felt secure behind the shield of her navy, and traditionally she had tried to keep clear of entangling alliances unless her own vital interests were at stake. Initially she had perhaps more sympathy with the Triple Alliance Powers of Germany, Austria and Italy. For centuries she had been the rival of France, and during the struggle for colonies in the nineteenth century they had frequently come into conflict. As late as 1898, for example, there was talk of war between Britain and France when they quarrelled over territory and competing claims at Fashoda in the Sudan. Britain was also fearful and suspicious of Russia, for her interests were threatened by the Russian advance against Turkey towards Constantinople, the Russian advance against Persia in the Middle East, and by Russian infiltration in Afghanistan on the borders of British India. On the other hand, Britain had strong links with Germany through the royal family, and many people in Britain admired the swift upsurge of nationalism that had seen Germany united and triumphant over the old enemy France. As one writer expressed it:

'That noble, patient, deep, pious and solid Germany should be at length welded into a nation and become queen of the Continent, instead of vapouring, vainglorious, gesticulating, quarrelsome, restless, and over-sensitive France, seems to me the hopefullest public fact that has occurred in my time.'

However, as the rival alliances built up their strength, British statesmen were forced to re-examine their traditional policies of keeping clear of Continental entanglements. Britain's position seemed increasingly dangerous, for if she was involved in a quarrel with one Power, then she might have to face that Power's allies as well. Her vulnerable position was highlighted during the Boer War (1899–1902), for almost every European country sympathised with the Boers and might have been tempted to send them aid if British naval power had not stood in the way. Even more serious perhaps was the fact that Germany began building a large navy in the closing years of the nineteenth century. German business leaders had long urged that she should have a powerful fleet to protect her commercial and colonial interests, and now the Kaiser was won over by their arguments. In 1898 and 1900 Navy Laws were passed in Germany providing for the construction of a powerful fleet which would, as the German Admiral Von Tirpitz put it, equip Germany for 'a battle in the North Sea against England'.

Increasingly conscious of the menacing situation that faced them, British statesmen were now convinced that they must seek to settle their disputes with the Continental countries and come to some agreement with one or other of the rival blocs. The old attitudes were strong enough, how-

Admiral Von Tirpitz

Empire would perish and be swept utterly away if our naval supremacy were to be impaired. It is the British Navy which makes Great Britain a great power. But Germany was a great Power respected and honoured all over the world, before she had a single ship.'

The negotiations and their break-down revealed clearly the growing rivalry and antagonism that had developed between Britain and Germany. Britain had formerly been the dominant commercial power, but now she found German merchants and goods penetrating her spheres of influence. Germany, for instance, became more influential in the Middle East, and her proposal to build a railway from Berlin to Baghdad seemed to threaten British interests and influence in that region. Britain was also alarmed by the growing military power of

ever, to ensure that the early moves were towards Germany. Thus in 1898 and again in 1899 Joseph Chamberlain, the British Colonial Secretary, tried to negotiate an Anglo-German agreement, but on both occasions the discussions broke down. The main stumbling block was Germany's determination to build a large navy, for Britain felt that such a navy could be directed only against herself. As Winston Churchill was to say, a navy was an absolute necessity for Britain, while it seemed to be a luxury for Germany:

'The purposes of British naval power are essentially defensive. There is, however, this difference between the British naval power and the naval power of Germany. The British Navy is to us a necessity, and, from some points of view, the Germany Navy is to them more in the nature of a luxury. Our naval power involves British existence. It is existence to us; it is expansion to them. We cannot menace the peace of a single Continental hamlet, no matter how great and supreme our Navy may become. But, on the other hand, the whole fortunes of our race and

European possessions in Africa

Germany and by the seemingly threatening ambitions and policies of the Kaiser. Germany, for her part, felt that Britain had outwitted her over the struggle for colonies in Africa and that Britain was trying to hold back her legitimate ambition to be a world power. 'England has treated herself well in matters of colonial territory,' declared one German commentator, 'yet if it is announced that Germany has acquired territory in the South Pacific or in the South of Africa a howl arises that Germany has acquired a strategic point which will command a British colony or trade route.' Such feelings spread through Germany, and travellers there noted a growing hostility to Britain and all things British:

'The place was alive with malice; its heart, fuelled with animosities, was continually bursting against Britain, which was to be outnumbered on land, outbuilt at sea, in fact outed everywhere.'

Japan

With the failure of the Anglo-German negotiations, Britain felt she was in an even more exposed position, and there was an increased determination among her statesmen that her isolation should be ended. Her first successful movement away from isolation, however was not towards a European country, but towards Japan in Asia. Japan had become a strong industrial, military and naval Power, and she had ambitions of extending her influence in Asia and the Pacific. This brought her into opposition to Russia who was expanding in this region, and since Britain was also alarmed at Russian ambitions, Japan and Britain were brought closer together. In 1902, therefore, the two countries signed a treaty whereby they declared they would be neutral if the other was involved in war with one country, but they would provide assistance if the ally was at war with two or more powers.

This Russian cartoon shows Britain and America pushing Japan into war with Russia

Secure in her alliance with Britain, Japan determined to deal with Russia. In 1904 war broke out between the two countries, and to the astonishment of the European Powers the Japanese inflicted a severe defeat on the Russians. She destroyed two great Russian fleets, and then in 1905 she captured Port Arthur. As a result of the war the Japanese gained Port Arthur and other territories, while the Russians withdrew from Korea and Manchuria. Japan was now clearly a powerful force in Asia, and she looked confidently forward to new advances in the Pacific and against China.

The Entente

Meanwhile in Europe Britain and France were making strenuous efforts to settle their traditional quarrels and differences. As Germany appeared ever more menacing and threatening to both countries, it seemed to statesmen in both Britain and France that they could no longer afford to remain enemies. In 1903 King Edward VII (1901–10) made a visit to France, and so successful was it that relations between the two countries improved markedly. In 1904 they made an agreement or entente which sought to remove some of the old points of dispute. This was not a formal alliance, but France recognised that Britain should hold a predominant position in Egypt, while Britain recognised France's claim to a dominant influence in Morocco.

First Moroccan Crisis

The Germans were astonished and alarmed by this coming together of Britain and France. They had assumed that the enmity between the two countries was so great that such an agreement was impossible, and indeed this belief helps to explain why they did not try harder to come to terms with Britain in 1898. They now determined to undo the damage by smashing the Entente and prising the two countries apart, and to secure this objective they engineered a crisis in Morocco. In 1905 the Kaiser visited Tangiers and spoke of recognising the independence of Morocco. He demanded an international conference to discuss the situation, but when the conference met at Algeciras in 1906

Kaiser Wilhelm in Tangiers, 1905

Edward VII in Paris, 1903

the British gave their full support to the French. Thus instead of weakening the Entente, the Germans had merely succeeded in strengthening it, for representatives of Britain and France met to discuss military and naval cooperation if war should break out. At the Conference, too, most of the other Powers also supported France, and she, together with Spain, was given responsibility over the Moroccan police and customs.

The Entente between Britain and France led on a few years later to an agreement between Britain and Russia, for it was natural that France should wish to bring them together. She used her influence in both countries, and in 1907 an Anglo-Russian Entente was signed. By its terms Russia agreed to cease her interference in Tibet and Afghanistan, while Persia was divided into three zones: the northern zone to be under Russian influence; the southern zone within the British sphere of influence; and a neutral zone in the middle. Thus by 1907 a Triple Entente had been formed between Britain, Russia and France which in a sense counter-balanced the Triple Alliance of Germany, Austria and Italy.

Naval race

Although the Triple Entente was certainly not a definitive and binding alliance for Britain, she was increasingly brought closer to France and Russia as the naval race between Germany and herself intensified. In 1904 Britain had replied to the growing strength of the German Navy by forming a Home Fleet with a base at Rosyth in Scotland. In 1905 a new stage was reached when Britain began building the first dreadnought, a swift battleship with ten 12-inch guns that threatened to make earlier battleships obsolete. Germany also started to build dreadnoughts, and she began widening the Kiel Canal in 1906 to allow them to pass from the Baltic to the North Sea. Signs of the increasing tension appeared in 1908 when Admiral Fisher, the British First Sea Lord, suggested that Britain should 'Copenhagen' the German fleet before it became too strong – i.e. destroy it as the Danish fleet had been destroyed in 1807. A panic gripped Britain in 1909 when it was reported that Germany was building ahead of schedule, and there was a great popular demand for more battleships with the slogan, 'We want eight, and we won't wait'. A new accelerated programme was laid down by the Liberals, and this enabled Britain to retain her lead, with Britain

laying down eighteen dreadnoughts between 1909–12 as against Germany's nine. But the German threat continued to alarm the British authorities, and in 1912 she began transferring ships from the Far East and the Mediterranean to the North Sea. It was agreed with France that France would protect British interests in the Mediterranean, while Britain would defend the French Channel coast against possible German attacks. In this way Britain was being brought ever closer to France and dragged inexorably into the affairs of the Continent.

While the British were building Dreadnoughts and reviewing their mighty fleet at Spithead (opposite page), the Germans were building their own dreadnoughts (top, left), widening the Kiel Canal (top, right) and the Kaiser was personally involved in building up a highly disciplined, modern navy (bottom left).

agreements on disarmament and arms limitations, but both ended in failure. The armaments factories in the various countries, therefore, continued to pour forth great quantities of weapons of all sorts, and each country on the Continent strove to create a huge conscript army that could make use of all these arms. Germany's army was undoubtedly the most highly trained and efficient, and she had the ability to move a force of three and a half million men into the field. France and Russia sought to equal her, and by increasing the length of conscript service they planned that France would have a field army of three and a half million men and Russia one of four million men. Britain had no conscription and her regular army was much smaller, but in 1907 the Secretary of War, R.B. Haldane, began a reorganisation to create a small but highly trained Expeditionary Force of six divisions (c. 150,000 men) which could be speedily mobilised in an emergency and might be sent overseas.

Military preparations

The Naval Race was, of course, only one aspect of a gigantic arms race that involved all the Great Powers. Two Conferences were held at the Hague in 1899 and in 1907 in an attempt to secure

The military plans

Each country, too, had prepared elaborate military plans to win victory in any future war. Most military leaders accepted the doctrines of

The German Crown Prince at the head of his regiment, the Death's-head Hussars

Clausewitz, the great German military theorist, who had stressed the importance of the swift offensive and of concentrating large forces at vital areas to overwhelm the enemy:

'Superiority in numbers is the most important factor in the result of a combat. The destruction of the enemy's military force is to be sought for principally by great battles, and the chief object of great battles must be the destruction of the enemy's main force.'

The Schlieffen Plan

These doctrines of Clausewitz had seemed to be vindicated during the Franco-Prussian War (1870–1) when the Prussian forces had won a speedy victory by a swift, decisive offensive. Now all the generals began making plans for similar swift attacks on their potential enemies. Perhaps the most famous of all these plans was that designed by General Schlieffen, Chief of the German General Staff, in order to allow Germany to cope with a war on two fronts, on the East against Russia and the West against France. He planned for the bulk of the German Army to be flung against France, while small defensive forces would face the Russians in

the East. After the French had been crushed, the Army would be transferred to the East to deal with the Russians:

'The whole of Germany must hurl itself against one opponent, the one who is the strongest, most powerful, most dangerous; this cannot but be France. The Russian army, destined to serve against Germany, will not march on Galicia before the die has been cast in the west, and the fate of Austria will be decided, not on the Bug, but on the Seine.'

By 1905 Schlieffen had developed his plans for the great attack on France that would crush her in six weeks. There were strong French forts on the frontier between the two countries, and so he decided on a great outflanking movement by swinging through Belgium into northern France. He proposed placing massive forces on the right wing of the German army for this outflanking attack, with only minimum forces on the defensive in the centre and left:

'The mass of the western force – seven armies with sixty-nine divisions, twenty-two Landwehr (territorial) brigades – was to advance first against the Dunkirk-Verdun line in a vast leftward wheel with Metz as its pivot. In Lorraine only one army was to be retained with ten divisions. On the upper Rhine only three and a half brigades were to remain. Upper Alsace was to be left undefended. The relative strengths of the right and left wings of the army was approximately seven to one.'

In the years after 1905 the plan was modified to provide stronger defence forces on the left and centre, and thus there was now a ratio of three to one in the relative strengths of the right to left wings instead of the original seven to one. The details were all worked out, the mobilisation of the army and reserves was planned down to the last man, and elaborate railway timetables were drawn up to transport the various units at top speed to the French and Belgian frontiers. So complex indeed were the details of the plan that once it had been initiated it would prove extremely difficult to bring it to a halt. More and more it became evident that if a German victory was seen to depend on the success of the Schlieffen Plan, then nothing could be allowed to halt it or to endanger it once a crisis had reached a certain point.

Other countries, too, developed their plans for offensive operations. The French, for example, had their famous Plan XVII which envisaged an all-out attack in the south into Germany. Russia drew up plans for offensives against Austria in Galicia and against Germany in East Prussia. Britain, for her part, prepared to send the British Expeditionary Force (B.E.F.) to France, and detailed arrangements were made for carrying the troops and their equipment to the French Channel ports. In each case the generals stressed the importance of swift action, and they insisted that their plans should not be jeopardised by the politicians delaying too long in any international crisis that might lead to war.

International crises

Bosnia-Herzegovina The dispute over Morocco in 1905–6 had been such a crisis, and in the years up to 1914 there were to be a number of other dangerous international incidents. One occurred in the Balkans in 1908, for example, when Austria annexed the provinces of Bosnia-Herzegovina. Austria had been administering these former Turkish territories since 1878, but her decision to take them over completely was a blow to Serbia who looked on the Bosnians as her kindred Slavs who would one day join with Serbia. The Serbs appealed to Russia for assistance, and there seemed a danger of war, for Russia was herself alarmed and angered at this extension of Austrian influence in the Balkans. But when Germany made it clear in 1909 that she would give her fullest support to Austria, Russia backed down. She had been weakened by her defeat in the war with Japan in 1904–5, but now she began to reorganise her army so that she would not be so humiliated again.

Agadir: the Second Moroccan Crisis The next dangerous international incident occurred once again in North Africa. French troops were sent to Morocco in 1911 to quell a rebellion there, and in reply Germany sent a warship, the *Panther*, to the port of Agadir. In the ensuing crisis Germany did

The *Panther*

not receive strong support from her allies Austria and Italy, and she had eventually to accept a settlement whereby Morocco became a French protectorate and in return Germany received territory from the French in the Congo. Germany had also been taken aback by the warlike talk of Britain who had been alarmed at this use of German naval power in a strategic area. Lloyd George declared:

'I believe that it is essential in the highest interests not merely of this country, but of the world, that Britain should at all hazards maintain her place amongst the Great Powers of the world. I would make great sacrifices to preserve peace. But if a situation were to be forced upon us in which peace could only be preserved by the surrender of the great and beneficent position Britain has won by centuries of heroism and achievement, by allowing Britain to be treated where her interests were vitally affected as if she were of no account in the Cabinet of nations, then I say emphatically that peace at that price would be a humiliation intolerable for a great country like ours to endure.'

The Balkan Wars In 1912–13 attention was once more switched to the Balkans when war broke out between Turkey, on the one side, and Serbia, Bulgaria and Greece, on the other. The Balkan states were victorious, and Turkey was driven out of most of her European territories; but the victorious powers now quarrelled amongst themselves and in a second war Bulgaria was defeated by Greece, Romania and Serbia. All this had the effect of strengthening Serbia, whilst weakening Turkey and Bulgaria, countries who had become associated with Germany. Austria felt that her influence in the Balkans was threatened by the growth of Serbian power, and more than ever she considered Serbia as a menace to the survival of her Empire.

Sarajevo

These succeeding international crises had placed increasing strains on the European system. Each of the rival blocs suffered reverses, the Germans over Morocco and the Balkan Wars, the Russians over the Bosnia-Herzegovina question, and these reverses made them more determined than ever to be successful in the future. And then into this highly inflammable situation a new crisis burst in the summer of 1914. On 28 June the Archduke Franz Ferdinand, the heir to the Austrian throne, and his wife were assassinated by a Bosnian Serb while

The Balkan Wars 1912–13

The arrest of Princip, the assassin of Archduke Franz Ferdinand

visiting Sarajevo, the capital of Bosnia. Austria immediately blamed Serbia, and on July 23 she presented an ultimatum to Serbia demanding that the guilty persons should be punished and that Serbia should clear terrorists out of her lands. Serbia accepted most of the points of the ultimatum, but she refused to agree to the demand that Austrian officials should be involved in the suppression of anti-Austrian propaganda within Serbia. Austria now ordered partial mobilisation, and on 28 July she declared war on Serbia. The Austrian leaders, it seemed, were determined to seize this opportunity of crushing the Serbian threat to the Empire once and for all.

The fears and expectations that surrounded the whole network of alliances now came into play. Germany felt obliged to give her full support to Austria, for she was her only really reliable ally. Russia could not fail the Serbians as she had done in 1908–9, for she would thereby lose all influence in the Balkans. Russia had ordered partial mobilisation on 20 July, and when Austria declared war on Serbia she ordered full mobilisation on 31 July. Germany could not stand idly by while Russia mobilised on her frontiers, and on 31 July she sent an ultimatum to Russia demanding that she should demobilise her forces. Russia refused, and on 1 August Germany declared war on Russia. Now the German war plans came into operation, for all her preparations were geared towards an attack on France. For a time the Kaiser spoke of switching his armies to the East against Russia, but his generals convinced him that this was impossible. Accordingly the German war machine began rol-

BRAVO, BELGIUM!
Germany is shown here as a bully, threatening 'gallant little Belgium'

ling, and on 3 August she declared war on France. On 2 August Germany demanded free passage for her troops through Belgium, and when this was refused, German troops crossed the Belgian frontier on the morning of 4 August.

Britain

For a time it seemed doubtful if Britain would be dragged into the conflict. As the crisis deepened towards the end of July, she began mobilising her navy and army, but she had no firm agreement with France or Russia that would automatically involve her taking part. Indeed many of the Cabinet were quite opposed to Britain entering the War, but when Germany invaded Belgium, the Cabinet and public opinion swung firmly against Germany and in favour of intervention. On 4 August an ultimatum was sent to Germany demanding that her troops should be withdrawn from Belgium. No positive response had been received when the ultimatum expired at midnight, and Britain, too, was at war. *The Times* on 5 August summed up the reasons for Britain's decision:

'We are going into the war that is forced upon us as the defenders of the weak and the champions of the liberties of Europe. We are drawing the sword in the same cause for which we drew it against Philip II, against Louis XIV, and against Napoleon. It is the cause of right and honour, but it is also the cause of our own vital and immediate interests. The Netherlands and Belgium largely owe their independent existence to the instinct we have ever felt and ever acted upon – that on no account whatever can England suffer the coasts of the North Sea and of the narrow seas over against her to be at the command of a great military monarchy.'

And so all the preparations, alliances and crises had at last brought about the disaster which had been dreaded for so long. Each country was convinced that its enemies were the aggressors and that it had no real alternative but to fight for its honour and its vital security. Germany believed that she had been encircled and threatened by her enemies, while Austria considered that she was fighting for her very existence. Russia was convinced that she must intervene to protect Serbia if she were to retain her status as a Great Power, while France knew that if Russia were defeated she would be powerless against a victorious and strengthened Germany. Britain and other countries felt that

Germany was bent on the domination of the Continent, and her invasion of Belgium (and Austria's attack on Serbia) convinced many that they were ruthless conquerors with no sympathy for the small and weak. Later there would be arguments and disputes about who was most to blame for the war, but for the moment each nation entered the struggle convinced of the rightness of its cause and determined to win victory.

Exercises   Chapter Three

1 a) Show how Europe had become divided into two armed camps in the years before 1914. *5*
   b) Explain how any one international crisis in the years between 1905–13 brought about a danger of war in Europe. *5*
   c) What military plans and preparations had been made by Germany to secure victory in any war that might break out? *5*
   d) What steps had been taken by Britain to prepare her navy and army for war in the years before 1914? *5*
   (20)

2 The following is an extract from a book written by Winston Churchill.
'The purposes of British naval power are essentially defensive. There is, however, this difference between the British naval power and the naval power of Germany. The British Navy is to us a necessity, and, from some points of view, the German Navy is to them more in the nature of a luxury. Our naval power involves British existence. It is existence to us; it is expansion to them. We cannot menace the peace of a single Continental hamlet, no matter how great and supreme our Navy may become. But, on the other hand, the whole fortunes of our race and Empire would perish and be swept utterly away if our naval supremacy were to be impaired.'

   a) Why, according to the writer, was a powerful navy a 'necessity' to Britain? *2*
   b) Why did Germany seek to expand her navy in the early years of the twentieth century? *4*
   c) Outline the main stages of the Naval Race that emerged between Britain and Germany. *5*
   d) What other quarrels and disputes affected relations between the two countries at this time? *4*
   e) How important was naval rivalry with Germany in bringing about Britain's entry into the First World War? *5*
   (20)

3 Imagine you are a British tourist who has been present at Sarajevo on 28 June 1914 and has witnessed the assassination. Write a letter home to a friend giving an account of the events and your views on the significance and possible consequences of the assassination. (20)

Chapter Four

The first great battles

The contestants

By the early days of August 1914, there were seven countries engaged in the War: Russia, France, Britain, Belgium and Serbia comprising what came to be known as the Allies; and Germany and Austro-Hungary the Central Powers. Italy refused to join the fighting, claiming that her treaty with Germany and Austria was defensive and that Austria had started the War. By the end of the War some thirty countries were to be engaged on one side or the other, but for the moment the crucial first battles would be fought by the armies of these initial contestants.

In a strange way the War was greeted with almost a sense of relief in most of these countries, for it seemed as if the people were glad that the long years of anxiety and crises were ended. In all countries, too, there was a tendency to forget their own internal quarrels and to unite to face this great trial of strength. For example, various socialist parties now switched to give their full support to the War, even although a short time before many of them had been talking of refusing to serve against their fellow-workers in a capitalist struggle. In Britain the internal disputes and struggles that had wracked the country were ended almost at a stroke. Most of the trade union movement supported the War, the suffragettes halted their campaign and offered their services, while the Irish question was shelved as the leader of the Irish Nationalists in Parliament pledged support and as men from both sides in the Irish struggle volunteered for the British Army.

The armies march

To any independent observer of the European scene in the early days of August 1914, the Continent must indeed have appeared a strange and rather frightening place. In all the countries involved there was wild excitement and enthusiasm, and great crowds gathered in the capitals to cheer their leaders and the outbreak of war.

In France

'the news spread like wild-fire through the whole of Paris, and within a short time large crowds of men were marching arm in arm through the main streets singing the Marseillaise. Paris now rings with the famous shout, "To Berlin". The enthusiasm of the country knows no bounds.'

In Vienna

'a crowd demonstrated in front of the Foreign Office while groups collected around the various statues of national heroes waving black and yellow flags and singing the Austrian National Anthem.'

In Berlin

'patriotic demonstrations continued all day outside the Imperial Palace. At half past six the German Emperor and Empress appeared on the balcony and received a great ovation.'

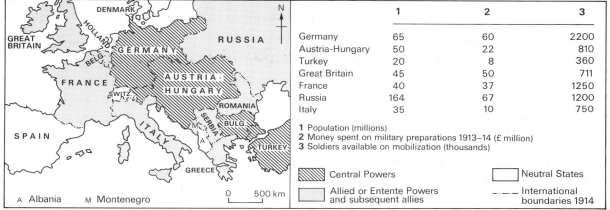

	1	2	3
Germany	65	60	2200
Austria-Hungary	50	22	810
Turkey	20	8	360
Great Britain	45	50	711
France	40	37	1250
Russia	164	67	1200
Italy	35	10	750

1 Population (millions)
2 Money spent on military preparations 1913–14 (£ million)
3 Soldiers available on mobilization (thousands)

▨ Central Powers		☐ Neutral States
▨ Allied or Entente Powers and subsequent allies		–··– International boundaries 1914

A Albania   M Montenegro   0 ___ 500 km

The combatants in the First World War

Everywhere on the Continent, too, the armies were assembling and marching off to war. Soldiers and reservists reported to their appointed centres, and everywhere there was great cheering and flag-waving as the troops marched through the towns and cities and off to the railway stations and embarkation points. Great crowds turned out to speed them on their way, and women pressed forward to hang flowers and garlands on the soldiers and their rifles. Then as the crowded troop trains thundered on their way to the various fronts, people would gather at stations and sidings to cheer on the smiling and waving soldiers.

War in the West; the Schlieffen Plan

From Germany the main movement of troops was westwards to the great railroad assembly points that had been built near the Belgian and Luxembourg borders. The initial operations went like clockwork, as the troops, the regiments and the divisions moved to their allotted places. They were organised into seven great armies, with the first five armies in the north directed to swing round through Belgium and northern France in a great encircling movement that would eventually trap and destroy the French armies against the Swiss frontier. The Germans struck forcefully into Belgium on 4 August, and their troops were soon advancing at roughly thirty miles a day. But soon they were encountering difficulties, for the Belgians destroyed the railway lines as they fell back and this interrupted the German supplies. The Germans were also delayed by the Belgian fortress of Liege for twelve days, but they captured Brussels on 20 August and pushed the Belgian army aside into Antwerp. Now the German war machine rolled on into France and towards Paris.

The delay at Liege and the brave resistance of the Belgians had won time for the French to send troops from the south to the north and for the B.E.F. under General Sir John French to arrive in France. The British plans for despatching the Expeditionary Force had also worked very smoothly, and four divisions consisting of about 100,000 men had been assembled. The movement of troops started on 9 August, with a complex operation of special trains taking the soldiers from Aldershot and other depots throughout the country. The first troop train arrived at Southampton on the morning of 10 August, and from there the first units of the B.E.F. were taken by sea to the French port of Le Havre. The initial operation was completed by 17 August, and the B.E.F. moved into Belgium to-

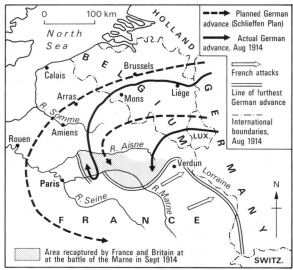

The German attack (compared with the Schlieffen Plan)

wards the town of Mons. There they took up defensive positions and awaited the advancing German First Army under General von Kluck. The Kaiser had learnt of the arrival of the British troops, but his orders to von Kluck showed that he did not rate them very highly:

'It is my Royal and Imperial Command that you address all your skill and all the valour of my soldiers to exterminate the treacherous English and walk over General French's contemptible little army.'

On 23 August von Kluck's advance guards stumbled into the positions of Britain's 'contemptible little army'. The Germans attacked with great masses of troops organised in solid formations and observing rigid discipline:

'The fusiliers saw something which caused them to blink unbelievingly and push the safety catches on their rifles forward with hands that

44

German infantry advancing through open country

The British Gattling machine-gun

shook; a solid mass of grey was coming over the skyline in columns of four; they advanced shoulder to shoulder and so unhurriedly as if they had been on a ceremonial parade.

'On this day of slaughter fusiliers found that they were killing effortlessly. It was, in truth, scarcely possible to miss. As the leading files of closely packed German infantry fell, those behind them pressed ever forward; some broke into a run, shouting wildly; others crouched behind dead comrades and returned the fire; and still they continued to fall – some dead before they hit the ground, some who would assuredly die before nightfall, some maimed for life; and all the time machine-guns pumped long bursts of fire into the screaming, struggling grey mass in front of them.'

This pattern of mass attacks in precise order had been what had been advised by the military planners before the War, but in the face of modern rifle and machine-gun fire it proved disastrous. The British Army, moreover, had been specially trained in rapid rifle fire, and so great had been their firepower that the Germans believed that the British units had many more machine-guns than they actually possessed. Faced with such losses and such

a deadly curtain of fire, therefore, the Germans abandoned their frontal attacks at Mons and brought up artillery to pound the British positions. They then attacked in short, rapid rushes, and at the same time they began outflanking and encircling the British defences. Heavily outnumbered and in danger of being surrounded as the forces on their flanks gave way, the British army was forced to retreat from Mons. Pursued by the overwhelmingly superior German forces, the B.E.F. fell back through northern France, all the time fighting desperate rear-guard actions and sometimes marching up to forty miles a day. But although it often seemed as if they would be encircled and destroyed, the skill and discipline of the soldiers saved them from complete disaster and preserved the B.E.F. as a fighting force in the field.

Battle of the Marne

As the British reeled back from Mons in their epic retreat, and as the great French armies on their flanks were forced back by the onslaught of the German right wing, it seemed that the Schlieffen Plan was proving successful. By the end of August advance units of the German Army came within fifty miles of Paris, and so dangerous seemed the situation that the French government moved to safety at Bordeaux. But in fact all was not going well with the German plans, for the delays caused by the Belgian resistance, the French recovery to switch troops to the north, and the fierce fight put up by the British at Mons and beyond had upset their timetable and delayed their advance. The Russians had also mobilised more quickly than expected, and when they launched an attack against East Prussia, vital German troops were removed from the Western Front and sent to the East. The German soldiers in France were also tired out after their long march and continuous fighting, while the French were able to use the railway system centred on Paris to switch round their forces from one sector to another as the situation developed.

A significant change of plan now occurred, for von Kluck, the commander of the German First Army on the right flank, had become worried as he seemed to lose contact with the German Second Army on his left. Accordingly the direction of his advance was altered to bring him closer in to the Second Army, and now he was heading east of Paris instead of to the west as in the original Schlieffen Plan. Thus instead of encircling Paris and outflanking the French forces in that region, the Germans now presented a vulnerable flank as they passed

Paris taxis ready to take troops to the Marne

across the face of the city. General Joffre, the French commander in Paris, immediately seized his opportunity. After gathering all the available forces, including some units rushed from Paris in taxi-cabs, he launched a counter-attack on the River Marne on 4 September. There was a fierce and confused struggle, but after five days of fighting the Germans broke off and retired forty miles to defensive positions on the River Aisne. The Schlieffen Plan had failed, and the great German attempt to encircle and defeat the French armies had been foiled.

Meanwhile the French offensive in the south had also been defeated. As proposed under plan XVII the French army had lauched a series of attacks into German territory in Lorraine from 14 to 20 August. In this sector they had superiority in numbers, but although they advanced a short distance they suffered heavy losses and made little impression on the German defences. Then the German 6th and 7th Armies under Prince Rupprecht launched a counter-attack and drove them back from the ground they had gained. The great French dreams of a triumphant offensive that would bring swift victory had also been shattered.

The race to the sea

As with the collapse of Plan XVII for the French, so the failure of the Schlieffen Plan was a bitter blow for the Germans. Von Moltke, the German Commander in the West, was a broken man, and sadly he reported to the Kaiser: 'Your Majesty, we have lost the war.' He was replaced by General Falkenhayn, and the new commander sought to gain an advantage by consolidating his front on the Aisne and then seeking to outflank the Allies to the north and so capture the Channel ports of Calais and Boulogne. Since this move could have halted the flow of troops and supplies from Britain to

France, the Allies replied with a similar attempt to outflank the Germans. A race to the sea developed as the enemy armies sought to outflank each other, and there was fierce fighting throughout October and November 1914. Antwerp fell to the Germans, but at Ypres in Belgium the British and Belgian troops managed to halt the German advance along the coast. Ypres was a terrible and bloody battle in which there were some 50,000 British casualties, but it saved the Channel ports and prevented a German break-through. Here the old B.E.F. was practically destroyed, but its sacrifice had helped defeat the German plans of 1914. At Ypres both the Germans and the British fought with great courage and tenacity:

Digging trenches near Ypres. This countryside would soon be unrecognizable

> 'On the 11th November, after a preliminary bombardment of unparalleled intensity, the Germans launched the two brigades of the Prussian Guard, some 13,000 men of the picked soldiers of the German Army, pledged to victory or death. They came on magnificent in their steadiness, moving in mass formations as if on parade and dying methodically in ranks and companies. Despite their casualties, so vast were their numbers and such the momentum of their mass that they penetrated the British line at several points and passed through into the woods. A counter-attack was delivered which once more cleared the woods. There were deadly hand-to-hand grapples with revolver and bayonet, and dusk fell upon the victorious remnants of the British force still holding their positions, before which the Guard lay dead in wide piles, swathes and knots.'

By the end of 1914 the struggles of the rival armies in the West had reached deadlock. Both sides had lost well over half a million men as the machine-guns, rifles, artillery and high explosives took their grim toll in those fearsome summer and autumn battles. The armies of both sides began to dig in where they stood, and soon an elaborate network of trenches was constructed extending from the Channel coast to Switzerland. The war of movement died down, and the great armies faced each other across No Man's Land from their opposing trenches. The losses had been so terrible that there was talk of a negotiated peace, but neither side was ready to accept any compromise or anything other than complete victory after such losses and sacrifices.

War in the air

The campaign of 1914 on the Western Front also saw the beginnings of air warfare. At the outbreak of war Britain had about two hundred military aircraft, with France having about the same and Germany rather more, and on 13 August three squadrons of the Royal Flying Corps (R.F.C.) with thirty-seven planes flew from Dover to Amiens and Mauberge. The main British plane at this time was the BE2 which could fly at 112 kilometres an hour and climb to a height of 3200 metres, but most of the aircraft of 1914 were little more than 'contraptions of wood and canvas held together by wire'.

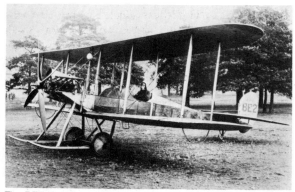

The BE2. A fighter during the early part of the war

Flying across the Channel in such planes was a great and perilous adventure where the pilots carried motor-car inner tubes as lifebelts in the event of forced landings in the water. In France the aircraft were used initially for reconnaissance and target spotting for artillery. They carried no mounted weapons, but some of the pilots had revolvers or rifles to fire at enemy aircraft. In the early days the R.F.C. supported the B.E.F. at Mons and on the retreat, and the information they provided helped to give the army information about the Germans' movements. Here are some extracts from the diary of Lieutenant W.R. Read who took part in these first air patrols:

'*25 August* Yesterday the Germans had a victory at Mons. I went off at 11 am with Jackson as passenger. All our troops were in retreat. The whole of the French cavalry were retiring on Cambrai. Returned from reconnaissance at 1 pm and at 3.30 orders came to move to St Quentin.

'*26 August* Off on reconnaissance at 7 am with Jackson to report on engagements in the Le Cateau and Espignol area. Le Cateau was in flames. We were shelled by anti-aircraft guns so I kept at 4,500 feet (1370 metres).

'*3 September* A rather disastrous day. On coming back from reconnaissance I smashed my new Henri on landing. The engine "chucked it" at a critical moment, and we did a complete somersault. I got a broken nose and damaged knees, and Major Moss, the observer, had his back badly bruised. The machine was absolutely broken up. I have broken up two machines in a week.

'*5 September* The Germans are moving east and appear to be ignoring Paris for the time being. It seems to be the idea of the French, having brought the Germans round to Paris, to cut them off and round them up.

'*8 September* News that we have driven back the Germans. They are now retreating as fast as they advanced.'

The Eastern Front

Meanwhile great and costly battles were also taking place on the Eastern Front. The Russians had advanced into East Prussia on 17 August, and their army of twenty two divisions inflicted a defeat on the German army of nine divisions, and the Germans were forced to retreat to the Vistula. At this point the Germans switched troops from the Western Front to the East, and a new commander, General Hindenburg, was appointed, with Ludendorff as his Chief of Staff. The Germans counter-attacked at the end of August, and in two great battles at Tannenberg and the Masurian Lakes they routed the Russians. Over 500 Russian guns were captured, while some 250,000 Russians were killed or taken prisoner.

In the south the Russians had attacked the Austrians, and quickly they overran the province of Galicia. They reached the Carpathian Mountains, but German reinforcements were sent to strengthen

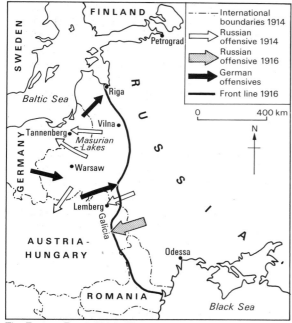

The Eastern Front, 1914–16

of the German High Seas Fleet, but the Germans remained in harbour. there were several small actions and forays with British ships attacking Heligoland Bight in August 1914 and destroying four German vessels, and German forces sailing across the North Sea to bombard Yarmouth in November and Scarborough and Whitby in December. Britain also suffered serious losses in home waters when three battlecruisers were sunk by a submarine in September and the battleship *Audacious* was sunk by a mine in October. Yet by the end of the year Britain had imposed an effective control over the North Sea and a blockade on Germany. She had been able to transport troops and supplies safely to France without any interference from the enemy; and from her naval bases at Scapa Flow and on the south coast of England she was able to control shipping entering or leaving the North Sea by the Channel or by the passage between Scotland and Norway. Germany could obtain supplies through neutral Holland or from Scandinavia and the Baltic, but already Britain was beginning to exert a stranglehold on her sea-borne trade.

On the wide oceans of the world, too, the strength of the British Navy was having its effect. At the outbreak of war there were several German naval vessels and armed raiders at large on the high seas, and some of them like the *Emden* sank many

the Austrian resistance and there the defences held. As the year ended the fighting died away, and on the Eastern Front, too, a kind of trench warfare appeared. In Serbia the Austrian invasion had failed, and all Austrian troops had been withdrawn from that country by the end of 1914. The pressure of the Russian armies against Austria had prevented her from concentrating large enough armies against Serbia to crush her.

War at sea

At sea many had expected there to be a great naval battle in the North Sea between the British and German fleets, but no such battle occurred in 1914. The British Grand Fleet took up station at Scapa Flow in the Orkney Islands to await the emergence

The *Emden*

The *Emden* after its destruction by the British

German report in their official war news showed how bitterly they resented this cooperation between Britain and an Asiatic country:

> 'Woe to you, Japan! England has betrayed the white races in the surrender of Tsing Tau to the Japanese. There is no honour for England or Japan in having taken Tsing Tau, which was defended by only 6,000 Germans, with a tenfold superiority after ten weeks' siege.'

Allied vessels, but by the end of the year they had been trapped and destroyed. A German cruiser squadron won a victory over a weaker British force at Coronel off Chile in November, but it was itself destroyed at the Falkland Islands in December. By this time the British Navy had gained complete control of the world's oceans and seas: her own trade and commerce were fully protected, while Germany's shipping had been sunk or driven into port, and her supply lines and communications had been cut. In addition Britain was in a position to send troops and supplies to any theatre of war in any part of the world.

Colonial struggles

The Allied control of the seas placed the German overseas colonies in a vulnerable position, and their possessions in Africa and the Pacific soon came under attack. Togoland in Africa was conquered by the end of August, while all the German possessions in the Pacific had fallen by the end of the year. Japan joined the Allies on 22 August, and she swiftly took over the Marianas, the Carolines and the Marshalls. In September a force of 22,000 Japanese and 1,750 British troops launched an attack on the German fortress of Tsing Tau which guarded the harbour of Kiao-chow in China. After a siege of ten weeks the German garrison of 6,000 men was forced to surrender in November. The

Turkey

The entry of Turkey into the war on 31 October 1914, on Germany's side, however, did help to compensate Germany for the reverses she had experienced in her overseas territories. Before the War Turkey had been brought within the German sphere of influence, and German army and naval officers had helped reorganise the Turkish forces. For a time the Turks hesitated, but the appearance of two German warships, the *Goeben* and *Breslau*, in Turkish waters decided the issue. The Turks officially took over the German ships, and these began attacking Russian ports in the Black Sea. Their major campaign in 1914 was in the Caucasus where in November they planned a great assault on the Russians. They were defeated and thrown back by the Russians, however, and over 75,000 Turkish soldiers perished in the battle or in the freezing conditions in the mountains of the Caucasus.

The situation at the end of 1914

As the first year of the war drew to a close, the various Powers could take stock and assess the outcome of all their hopes and plans. All countries had suffered enormous casualties, and the glib hopes they all had had of a swift and decisive offensive leading to complete victory had collapsed.

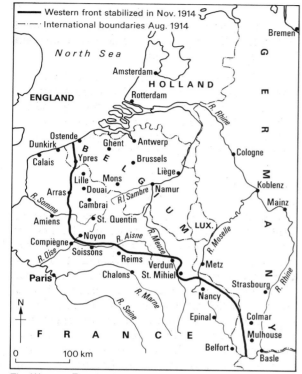

Key:
— Western front stabilized in Nov. 1914
–·– International boundaries Aug. 1914

North Sea

ENGLAND

HOLLAND
Amsterdam
Rotterdam

Bremen

R. Rhine

Cologne

Ostende
Dunkirk
Calais
Ypres
Arras
R. Somme
Amiens
Compiègne
R. Oise
Paris

Ghent
B
E
L
G
Lille
Douai
Cambrai
St. Quentin
Noyon
Soissons
Reims
Chalons
R. Marne
R. Seine

Antwerp
Brussels
Liège
Mons
Namur
R. Sambre
LUX.
R. Aisne
R. Meuse
Verdun
St. Mihiel
Nancy
Epinal

G
E
R
M
A
N
Y

Koblenz
Mainz

R. Moselle
Metz
Strasbourg
R. Rhine

Colmar
Mulhouse
Belfort
Basle

F R A N C E

N

0   100 km

The Western Front at the end of 1914

But each side could count its gains as well as its losses, and the colossal nature of the struggle and their casualties had not brought any of them to sue for peace. Already the leaders were making their plans for the following year, and everywhere they were calling upon their peoples for further efforts and sacrifices so that victory could be won in the coming campaigns.

Exercises Chapter Four

1 a) Outline the main stages of the German attack on France in August 1914. *8*

b) Show how the Germans came to be defeated by the Allies at the first battle of the Marne. *7*

c) Discuss the view that 'Germany lost the War at the Marne'. *5*
(20)

2 The following is an extract from orders sent by the Kaiser to von Kluck, commander of the German First Army in August 1914.
'It is my Royal and Imperial Command that you address all your skill and all the valour of my soldiers to exterminate the treacherous English and walk over General French's contemptible little army.'

a) Give details of the British force (the B.E.F.) described by the Kaiser as a 'contemptible little army'. *4*

b) Had the Kaiser any justification for regarding this force as an insignificant one? *3*

c) Give a brief outline of the means whereby the British force had come to be facing the Germans at Mons. *4*

d) Describe the action that followed between the British and German forces at Mons. *5*

e) How important a part did the B.E.F. play in defeating the German plans to conquer France? *4*
(20)

3 Imagine you are a German *or* a British soldier who had been mobilised and sent to the early campaigns in Belgium and France. Write a letter home in late December 1914 describing your experiences. *(20)*

4 'It'll all be over by Christmas.' Imagine you are a British leader who made the above prediction in August 1914. Now at the end of 1914 you are required to write a newspaper article explaining why your prediction went wrong and giving your assessment of the existing military situation. *(20)*

Chapter Five

Widening conflict

Trench warfare

As the rival generals looked out over the battlefields at the beginning of 1915, they were all too well aware that on many fronts the great battles of 1914 had resulted in a stalemate. The most obvious sign and symbol of the deadlock and stalemate that existed was the great system of trenches that had been erected across France and Belgium from the Channel to the Swiss frontier. The original impulse had come from the men's desire to find shelter from the sheer weight and firepower of modern arms and artillery, for only in underground positions could the soldiers have any real hope of surviving. Initially the armies had dug trenches where they stood as the fighting died away towards the end of 1914, but steadily the trench systems became more elaborate and complex. And all the time these trench systems provided an ever more formidable obstacle to the opposing armies if they wished to advance and attack.

Normally there were several lines of trenches on either side, the front line, the second line and the reserve lines, with communication trenches connecting the rear areas with the front line. The trenches were not built in straight lines, but zigzagged back and forth to prevent the enemy sweeping a whole section with their fire. To the front lay an area of No Man's Land leading to the enemy's positions, sometimes only about thirty metres away. The front line trenches were upwards of six feet deep so that a man could walk upright, and on the bottom there were duckboards or strips of wood. On the forward facing wall there was a firestep for sentries and the soldiers when they were repelling an attack, while in the rear wall there were dugouts where men could rest or shelter from artillery bombardments. Sandbags were piled on the front edge of the trenches to form parapets with loopholes through which the soldiers could fire, while great coils of barbed wire up to fifteen metres thick were placed in front of the trenches to prevent the enemy breaking through. Conditions varied from one part of the front to another, with dugouts being much deeper and safer in some places than in others. The Germans were much more thorough in their trench building, and often they used concrete to build deep and relatively safe dugouts for their troops.

As the armies became more familiar with this strange type of warfare, a whole range of new tactics and weapons was adopted. Great batteries of artillery were brought up and stationed behind the lines, and these were used to pound the enemy trenches and communications. Hand grenades and trench mortars became essential weapons, since they allowed soldiers to lob missiles from cover into the opposing trenches, while sappers and engineers dug out tunnels so that mines might be exploded under the enemy positions. Great star shells were developed to light up No Man's Land, and suddenly a patrol or a working party repairing the barbed wire would be cruelly exposed to the guns of the enemy. Night patrols were sent out regularly into No Man's Land to collect information about the enemy, and sometimes there would be desperate hand to hand struggles there in the darkness. At all times, too, there was the constant danger from snipers whose sights were trained on the enemy trenches waiting for any unwary soldier to raise his head above the parapet. But still the battlefield was dominated by the machine-gun emplacements situated at intervals along the trench walls, for these could lay down a hail of fire if the enemy dared advance to attack a salient or to straighten out a bend in the line.

The plain fact was that by 1915 the defensive forces had gained the upper hand through the development of modern weapons. The artillery and the machine-guns could pour forth a murderous fire across No Man's Land, and together with the barbed wire entanglements in front of the trenches they presented a fearsome barrier to any attacking force. If an army advanced against them, whole swathes of soldiers would be mown down by the machine-gun fire, and as they halted at the barbed-wire they would literally be killed in great heaps and piles. Men carried wire cutters to force their way through, but too often they were struck down before they could use them. The trench system erected across France and Belgium, therefore,

presented a formidable military obstacle, and since it could not be outflanked it seemed that it could be breached only at a terrible cost in human life.

The conditions faced by the soldiers forced to live and fight in the trenches were quite appalling, and it became customary to send units there for only a limited tour of duty before they were allowed

British soldiers and their weapons

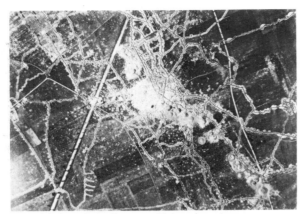

An aerial view of a battle area with trench systems

could send large military forces to tip the balance in their favour. The Germans, for their part, altered their whole strategy from that of 1914 and prepared to switch their main drive from the Western Front to the East. In France and Belgium they planned to remain on the defensive, and they began strengthening their lines against any possible Allied offensive. The Allies, however, were determined on a series of offensives to drive the enemy from French territory and to regain the rich industrial area of northern France. They had raised new units from their reserves and recruiting drives, while troops from the French and British Empires were now landing in France, among them the 1st Canadian Division which arrived in France in February 1915. With these new forces at their disposal, the allied generals did not feel that the trenches would hold them up for long. They were supremely confident that if they pounded the enemy positions with

a rest period at the rear. There was the ever present fear of an artillery bombardment and a horrible death as the trench walls caved in on top of them, the dangers of advancing in No Man's Land against the enemy machine-guns and barbed wire, and the ever constant dangers from snipers. Living conditions were often quite unspeakable with flooded trenches, bare rations of bully beef and hard biscuits, lice, fleas, rats, 'trench feet', and the constant reminder of death as buried corpses were exposed by artillery fire and as the bodies of friend and foe lay unburied in No Man's Land. Some men found the continual noise of the shellings quite unbearable, and the constant pounding struck at their nerves and pushed them to the verge of a break-down.

The Western Front in 1915

Faced with the trench systems and with the stalemate that had fallen upon the battlefields at the end of 1914, the generals and statesmen looked around anxiously for some means of winning the initiative: either by raising large new armies from within their own territories or by seeking out new allies who

The Western Front in 1915

artillery and if they poured enough men across No Man's Land they would be able to break through into a war of movement. The outcome was to be horribly different from their hopes and expectations.

The first Allied offensive of the year was launched by the French in the Champagne region from January to March 1915. The French generals had made optimistic predictions, but almost at once these were seen to be misplaced. Although a massive artillery bombardment was laid down, this did not destroy the German trench system and defences. The French suffered over 90,000 casualties to gain only a small area of ground of up to five miles. There was no break-through.

Other offensives throughout the year told the same story. On 10 March the British launched their first major attack at Neuve Chapelle, but this gained less than a square mile of ground for over 12,000 dead. In May the French attacked Vimy Ridge, but failed to capture the heights after suffering 100,000 casualties. They attacked here again in September, but once more they failed to capture the ridge. A great British effort was made against Loos in September, but although the initial assaults met with some success, it was brought to a halt after some 50,000 British casualties had been suffered. The Germans, on their side, did make one major assault at Ypres in April, and here they made use of the frightful weapon of poison gas. The surprise gained when they bombarded the Allied lines with capsules of the poison gas allowed them to make initial advances, but when they themselves ran into their own gas, they soon retreated, and this offensive, too, was a failure.

War in the air

Above the battlefields there were significant developments in the air war as both sides struggled to

Machine-gunners wearing gas helmets

bring out improved aircraft and as fresh squadrons were sent to airfields behind the fronts. Initially in 1914 both sides were evenly matched, with the Allies having about 240 planes as against the Germans' 230, but now there began a see-saw struggle as first one side and then the other gained the upper hand. In the spring of 1915 the advantage swung to the Allies as a Frenchman, Roland Garros, began fitting steel propellor blades which could deflect bullets. This enabled the Allies to mount machine-guns to fire straight ahead, and for some months they enjoyed a real dominance as they shot down many German observation aircraft. But soon a German aircraft designer, Anthony Fokker, replied by developing a method of synchronising the firing of a machine-gun through the propellors. With the new Fokker E1 plane with its machine-gun mounted directly in front of the pilot, the Germans gained control of the skies throughout the summer and autumn of 1915. Many Allied planes were shot down in this period, and British pilots jocularly described themselves as 'Fokker fodder'. But towards the end of the year the Allies also developed forward-firing and synchronised machine-guns, and with such aircraft as the British DH2 biplane they fought grimly with the German squadrons for air supremacy. These planes in France had become fighter aircraft, but elsewhere the rival airforces were developing the role and function of the bomber. Thus the R.F.C. made several attempts to bomb German railways in 1915, while from the beginning of the year German Zeppelin airships bombed London and Paris.

Italy

Although they had made little impression against the German defences in France in 1915, the Allies did receive some encouragement from the entry of Italy into the war on their side. Italy, as we have seen, had refused to take sides with her allies Germany and Austria in the quarrel over Serbia, and now the Allies persuaded her to join them in May 1915 by offering her territories at the expense of Austria (Secret Treaty of London). During the remainder of the year the Italians launched several offensives against the mountainous borderlands that formed the north-eastern frontier of Italy with Austria, but these were easily repulsed. The Austrians were entrenched in strong positions in the mountains and hilly country, and as the Italians attacked they were driven back with heavy losses.

The Eastern Front

The Allies' lack of success in the West was all the more serious and disappointing because of the fact that the Central Powers were achieving striking victories on the Eastern Front and in the Balkans. After halting the Russian offensives at the end of 1914, the Germans planned a great assault on the southern sector in Galicia. Using the railway systems of Germany and Austria they concentrated their forces, and by May the preparations were completed. The Russians were poorly supplied,

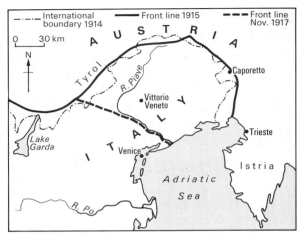

The Italian Front

and because of the greater distances involved their forces were spread more thinly over the front. Thus when the Austrians and Germans attacked, they were able to knock a great gap into the Russian lines. They advanced swiftly on a wide front some 500 miles broad, and the Russians were forced into a hurried retreat. The entire Russian front was driven back more than 200 miles, and by August Warsaw and the whole of Poland had fallen to the Germans. Some two million Russians were killed, wounded or taken prisoner, and this great victory had freed Austria and East Prussia from fear of a Russian invasion.

The Balkans

The Germans now focused their attention on the Balkans, and soon they had won equally resounding victories there. Impressed by the German victories against Russia, Bulgaria entered the war on the German side in October 1915, and she now joined Austria and Germany in a three-pronged assault on Serbia. The Serbians were no match for

Serbian soldiers and civilians in retreat

this combined force and they were quickly over-whelmed. By the beginning of 1916 Serbia had been crushed, and the position of the Central Powers was immensely strengthened. In effect they had control of the Balkans, and their communications with Turkey had been greatly improved. As for the Serbians, part of their army escaped over the mountains to Albania, and on this terrible march their troops endured immense hardships and suffering. They were forced to eat raw cabbages and candles and anything edible, and when they emerged from the mountains to the Adriatic they were described as 'dirty skeletons in rags'. They were taken by sea to Corfu, and many of them were so thin and emaciated that the nurses there could quite easily lift them up in their arms.

Turkey

Turkey was also involved in important campaigns during 1915, for her entry into the war had opened up the possibility of new fronts and theatres of war.

Some British leaders like Churchill and Kitchener indeed began to favour the alternative of launching attacks against Turkey that would by-pass the stalemate on the Western Front. One of the earliest moves was a British expedition to Mesopotamia, the modern Iraq. A British force from India had landed at Basra on the Persian Gulf in November 1914 to protect the oil pipe line there, and soon afterwards a combined British and Imperial force began advancing up the Tigris River towards Baghdad. They won several engagements and reached within 25 kilometres of Baghdad, but difficulties of supplies and increasing Turkish reinforcements forced them back to Kut on the Tigris. A force of some ten thousand men was besieged in Kut, and defiantly they held out for many months. Relief forces attempted to break through, but all were driven back. At length in April 1916 the garrison at Kut was forced to surrender. The British troops were taken to work on the Baghdad Railway, and there they suffered terribly from the heat, poor rations, disease and the cruelty of their Turkish guards. Some were tortured or thrashed to death, while many died of cholera or dysentery. In all, it is calculated, some two thirds of the British soldiers taken prisoner at Kut died before the war was over.

The Dardanelles

Early in 1915 another much more ambitious plan was drawn up by the Allied leaders against Turkey. This involved nothing less than a direct attack through the Dardanelles Straits to Constantinople to knock Turkey out of the war. Such an attack seemed much more attractive to men like Churchill and Kitchener than sending soldiers to 'chew barbed wire in Flanders', for they believed that a blow in this area could have a decisive influence on

ANZAC cove, Gallipoli

the War. The defeat of Turkey would open a front in the Balkans for an attack on Austria and Germany, while it would enable arms and supplies to be sent to Russia through the Black Sea.

The first stage of the campaign involved a naval attack on the Straits and their fortresses in March 1915. The guns of the fleet destroyed most of the Turkish fortresses, while the lighter guns from the Turkish forts did little damage to the armoured warships. It seemed that the naval force must break through to victory, but the loss by mines of three vessels, the *Irresistible*, *Ocean* and the French ship *Bouvet*, alarmed the commander and the War Cabinet in London, and it was decided to withdraw the fleet. British leaders were ever fearful that if they suffered heavy losses in warships they might lose their superiority over the German Navy. Yet probably this decision to withdraw was one of the real errors of the war, for the Turks and their German advisers were certain that they were on the verge of defeat.

A few weeks later in April 1915 the Allies attempted a combined military and naval attack on the Dardanelles to capture the Turkish forts and clear the way for the navy. British, French, Indian and Australian and New Zealand soldiers were landed on several beaches on the Gallipoli Peninsula, and eagerly they pushed inland and up the hills towards the Turkish positions. But the Turks had poured in reinforcements in the weeks since the naval attack, and they put up a fierce resistance. In one or two places the Allies came close to breaking through the Turkish positions and into the open country beyond, but the staff officers did not push home the attack. The assault was halted, and, as in France, both sides dug trenches and settled down to a stationary war. The Allies did launch several further attacks, but the Turks had sent in additional reinforcements and their lines held. Increasingly it became evident during the summer of 1915 that the Allies would not be able to break through, and to many military leaders their position seemed a most

58

The Dardanelles campaign

perilous one, perched as it was on a narrow strip of land and entirely dependent on supplies from the sea. At length it was decided to evacuate the army, and it was taken off in January 1916. The evacuation was carried out with great skill, and many clever devices were left in the trenches to trick the Turks into believing that they were still faced by a large Allied force.

Despite the success of the evacuation, the Dardanelles campaign was a serious reverse for the Allies. No new route had been opened up to send badly needed supplies to the Russians, and the grip of the Central Powers on the Balkans and the Middle East was firmer than ever. Some of the Allied troops from the Dardanelles were taken to reinforce an Allied garrison that had landed earlier in Salonika in Greece to protect that country against Bulgaria, but this force had little influence on the overall situation in the Balkans. Indeed the Germans were delighted to see some ¼ million Allied troops tied down there, and the Kaiser called the Salonika force his 'largest prisoner of war camp'.

War at Sea

At sea the British Navy continued with its vital tasks of imposing an effective blockade upon the enemy, preventing German warships from breaking out into the oceans, protecting the supply lines of Britain and her allies, transporting troops and supplies to all the theatres of war, and supporting military expeditions like the Dardanelles campaign. In the North Sea British control was exercised more effectively as minefields were laid in strategic areas and as patrols were mounted in the Channel and in the northern passage between Scotland and Norway. The German High Seas Fleet continued to remain in harbour, but a small engagement occurred at the Dogger Bank in January 1915 when a powerful British squadron under Sir David Beatty surprised a German raiding force of battle cruisers, cruisers and destroyers. Outnumbered, the Germans turned and fled for home, but their battle cruiser *Blücher* was sunk and the battle cruiser *Seydlitz* crippled. The British battle cruiser *Lion*

The Daily Mirror

CERTIFIED CIRCULATION LARGER THAN ANY OTHER PICTURE PAPER IN THE WORLD

No 3,609.   SATURDAY, MAY 8, 1915   **16 PAGES**   One Halfpenny

GIANT CUNARDER CROWDED WITH PASSENGERS CALLOUSLY SUNK
WITHOUT WARNING OFF THE IRISH COAST.

The announcement in the *Daily Mirror* of the sinking of the
Lusitania

had her steering damaged, but this clear victory was
a considerable boost to British morale.

The Germans, however, had much more success when they launched an intensified submarine
campaign in 1915 and declared that they would
attack any ship found in Allied waters as a retalia-
tion for the Allied blockade of Germany. They had
only twenty-seven submarines (U-boats) ready for
action, but they were soon inflicting serious damage
on their enemies, sinking some 59,000 tons of
Allied shipping in February and a peak of 186,000
tons in August. Among the victims was the British
liner *Lusitania* which was torpedoed in May in the
Irish Sea on a voyage from New York to Liverpool.
Over one thousand men, women and children were
drowned, among them many Americans, and the
tragedy aroused bitter anger in the United States.
Relations between Germany and the United States
deteriorated after this incident, and after several
American protests the Germans restricted their U-
boat campaign and ceased sinking neutral and
passenger ships at sight.

Colonies

With the Allies maintaining their overall control of
the seas, the Germans continued to experience
setbacks in their overseas colonies throughout
1915. In Africa the British conquered the Cameroons, while German South-West Africa was overrun by South African troops under General Botha
who had been fighting the British in the Boer War
only a few years previously. German East Africa
was also invaded, but here the resistance was much
stronger under the leadership of Colonel (later
General) Von Lettow-Vorbeck. He organised and
handled his German and native forces in a brilliant
manner, and throughout 1915 he managed to
repulse all the attacks that were launched against
the colony.

Position

As 1915 drew to a close, therefore, men could see
that the European conflict had been extended to
become a world-wide one. Great battles continued
on the Western and Eastern Fronts, but several
new theatres of war had been opened up. Clearly,
too, the advantage in many of the campaigns had lain
with the Central Powers, and their victories in
Russia, in the Balkans and the Dardanelles had
given them a strong wedge of influence throughout
the heartlands of Europe. Their successes in the

East also made possible the release of large numbers of skilled and confident troops who might be available for fresh campaigns in other theatres, and certainly the leaders of Germany and Austria might look forward with some confidence to the new year.

Among young and old, on both sides, the mood was still one of patriotic fervour

'One can look for miles and see no human being. But in those miles of country lurk (like moles or rats it seems) thousands, even hundreds of thousands of men, planning against each other perpetually some new device of death. Never showing themselves, they launch at each other bullet, bomb, aerial torpedo and shell. And yet the landscape shows nothing of all this, nothing but a few shattered trees and three or four thin lines of earth and sandbags; these and the ruins of towns and villages are the only signs of war anywhere visible.'

a) Explain how there had come to be these opposing lines of trenches in France as described in the passage.   *4*
b) Describe the structure and organisation of the trench systems.   *4*
c) In what ways did the soldiers in the trenches live like 'moles and rats'?   *4*
d) Give some examples of the means whereby the rival armies planned 'new devices of death' against each other.   *4*
e) Would you agree that the trenches provided a formidable military obstacle to the attacks of the enemy?   *4*
    (20)

Exercises   Chapter Five

1 a) With what objectives did Britain decide to attack Turkey through the Dardanelles Straits in 1915?   *6*
  b) Describe the naval and military attacks launched by the Allies at the Dardanelles, and explain why they failed.   *10*
  c) In what ways was this failure a serious reverse for the Allied war effort?   *4*
    (20)

2 The following is an extract from a description of the trenches in France written by a British officer.

3 Imagine you are an American who has been rescued from the *Lusitania*. Write a letter home to the United States describing your experiences and giving your reactions to the sinking.   *(20)*

4 'Gas!' Imagine you have been invalided out of the British army after the German gas attack at Ypres in 1915. Under the above title give an account of your experiences and your feelings about the fighting in France.   *(20)*

Chapter Six

Britain at war 1914–16

Attitudes to the war

The outbreak of war in Europe in 1914 was greeted, as we have seen, with tremendous enthusiasm in the countries involved, and in Britain, too, there was a great upsurge of patriotic feelings and excitement. As in other countries there was a fervent feeling that Britain was embarked on the noblest of causes, in her case to save gallant little Belgium and to rid the world of German aggression and militarism. A few individuals did oppose the War, but when they set up a Union of Democratic Control (U.D.C.) in December 1914 to secure a speedy negotiated peace, they received little support. The vast majority seemed to agree with the poet, Rupert Brooke, that 'Honour has come back, as a King, to Earth', while many young men echoed

the sentiments expressed by one writer when he declared: 'I feel nothing but gratitude to the gods for sending the war in my time.' Others felt the call to arms was almost a religious duty, a view expressed in dramatic terms by one commentator: 'The path of duty shone out in clearest light, and wherever it might lead us we had to go. It was the pillar of cloud by day and the pillar of fire by night. We must follow.'

Business as usual

Few people, however, had any real idea of the kind of war they had entered, and many even believed that their lives would continue much as before. In earlier wars the general life of the community had often not been greatly affected, and thus some individuals saw it all as an exciting adventure that would probably be over by Christmas. Harrod's, the famous London store, captured this mood when it placed the slogan, 'Business as Usual' in its window display, and many other shops and businesses took up the same cry. Almost at once, however, the people began to experience the impact of the War, for the country's trade was quickly disrupted by the conflict. Much of our food was imported at this time, and food prices were immediately affected, with imported meat rising by 1 penny (½p) and bread soaring from 5 pence (2p) to 8 pence (3½p).

Rupert Brooke, the war poet

D.O.R.A.

Even more drastic changes in people's lives were brought about by the passing of the Defence of the Realm Act on 8 August 1914 (D.O.R.A.). This gave the government special powers to help it prosecute the War, and heavy penalties and punishments were introduced for persons who might undermine the war effort. Anyone, for example, who communicated with the enemy or who interfered with the activities of the armed forces could be arrested and tried by court-martial. The government also took over control of the railways, docks and harbours, with similar powers to arrest and punish unauthorised persons who might trespass on what now became defence areas.

Recruits to the Services

Another dramatic impact of the War came with the movement of thousands upon thousands of men into the armed forces. On the outbreak of war, there were great scenes of enthusiasm throughout the United Kingdom as huge queues formed outside recruiting offices, and stories were told of complete football or cricket teams joining en masse. The government launched an effective recruiting campaign under the guidance of the War Secretary, Lord Kitchener, and compelling posters were put up on any available space. Women encouraged the men to volunteer by sometimes giving white feathers to any man not in uniform, while some of the popular music-hall songs had women singing:

'We don't want to lose you,

But we think you ought to go.'

As a result of these campaigns, some 500,000 volunteers had been recruited by the middle of September 1914, and by the beginning of 1915 the figure was well over one million. Everywhere there were gaps in the life of the country as more and

Thanks to the government campaign, there was no shortage of recruits

more men left their offices, factories or studies. The following extracts tell of the dramatic changes in London and Oxford, but such descriptions could have been repeated in every town and village in the land:

'From the crowd which throngs the earlier trains to London, between 7 o'clock and 9, only perhaps the station-master and porters could tell you how many familiar faces of the younger men are missing. The regular traveller is at most aware that certain of his personal acquaintances have gone; and beyond that he has the impression that on the platforms now there are more women and fewer men than there used to be.

'The talk in the compartments has become curiously military and geographical. Almost every day someone has received a letter dropped out of the unknown in an unstamped envelope covered with strange postmarks and uncouth cancellations, which is shown and passed round and discussed.

'The letters are short and roughly scrawled, dated only from 'The Front', 'At Sea', or 'In Base Hospital on Active Service'. Some men there are, too, who, as everybody knows, will receive no more such letters, and in their presence conversation about the war is carefully restrained.'

'The generous youth of England has rushed to arms, and the effect upon Oxford and Cambridge is strange indeed. At 11 or noon the streets are not now a-flutter with gowns hurrying to lectures; at 1 o'clock the groups in the gateways are scanty or none. The motor-bicycles are at the front, carrying despatches. The parks and the playing-fields are given up to drill, and football is confined to scratch matches got up once a week "to keep football going".

'By the end of November, all the oars of last year's Oxford eight, thirteen of the Rugby XV, nine of the cricket XI, eight of the Association XI, and all of the lawn tennis six had taken commissions. No wonder the university life languished.'

Women at war

The gaps left in so many places on the Home Front in Britain were soon being filled by women. Before the War women had worked in only a very small number of occupations, but now the needs of the War opened up many new opportunities to them. The leaders of the suffragettes, for their part, called off their campaign, and they encouraged their followers to take up war work. Soon women were occupying positions traditionally filled by men in industry, farming, transport, commerce and the professions. Some also served in special women's service corps, while others joined ambulance and nursing units serving in France and other theatres of war.

The ability of women to undertake all types of work astonished many observers at the time, and their contributions won all-round praise. Particularly admired were the munitions workers, for they faced real dangers with great courage and determination:

Women at work (and play) during the war

'The greatest honour seems to be due to those women who, knowing the risks, voluntarily undertake work in the danger houses of factories where high explosive (such as TNT) are handled. TNT produces a poison which is absorbed through the skin, and if it is absorbed it may have several results. Sometimes there is a skin eruption, short-lived but unpleasant. Most frequently the vulnerable part is the liver. Occasionally there are effects which make the supervisors believe that young women who handle TNT are sometimes permanently sterilized by it.

'As a protection the girls are supplied with respirators, veils and gloves. But the respirators irritate the skin round the mouth, and frequently rub it raw. As for the gloves, they are never worn by good workers. Overlookers agree that they cannot be worn, for example, in processes in which knots and loops have to be tied.

'The women who undertake this work are doing a very gallant service. Theirs is the highest courage, for many of them are nervous. The writer has seen a little group of new workers in tears because, although they had undertaken to work in the danger houses, they were scared when the moment came to go there. It is all the more to their honour that they were insisting through their tears that they "would be perfectly safe if they were careful".'

As women came to play a much more vital role in industry and commerce, so there was an important change in their fashions and social customs. The pre-war skirt had been extended to the ground, but by 1915 it had been raised to just below the calf. New types of underwear such as the brassière also became more popular at this time, and thus the war-time woman had a much greater freedom of action and movement. Many women, too, became much more independent as they came to live away from home and as they began to earn good wages.

New fashions

friend. But now with money and without men she is more and more beginning to dine out.'

In the war-time atmosphere, too, there seems to have been a new freedom given to women in their relations with the opposite sex. The ever-present sense of danger for the thousands of young soldiers and sailors helped to remove many of the old social customs and barriers, and people looked sympathetically on the feverish romances that occurred. There were many war-time marriages as girls married soldiers on their last leave before going to France, while the newspapers spoke of the 'war babies' born to young unmarried girls living near the great army camps and naval bases. Certainly many of these reports were exaggerated, but clearly there was a new freedom in war-time Britain that quite transformed the traditional position of women.

Germans and aliens

Another group in Britain who were especially affected by the outbreak of War were the Germans and other aliens in the community. The general enthusiasm for the War was accompanied by an upsurge of hostility towards the enemy, and this hostility was intensified as stories were spread in the press of atrocities being committed by the Germans in Belgium. Refugees from Belgium appeared in Britain, and the plight of these unfortunate people further inflamed feelings against the Germans. The German Kaiser was depicted as a foul monster, and soon the word 'German' came to represent everything evil and nasty.

Early in the War an Act was passed providing for the internment of enemy aliens of military age, but this was not enough for some sections of the population. Anyone with a German name came to be suspect, and there was a campaign to root out

Before the war women and girls of the middle classes would have been chaperoned or accompanied by a male companion in public places, but now this custom had to be abandoned:

'The wartime business girl is to be seen any night dining out alone or with a friend in the moderate-priced restaurants in London. Formerly she would never have had her evening meal in town unless in the company of a man

Rioters attacking a German shop in the east end of London

Air raid damage. All that was left of 45, Edridge Road, Croydon

from public life anyone who had ever had any connection with Germany. This campaign reached its climax when the First Sea Lord, Prince Louis of Battenberg, was forced to quit his office because he had German origins. There were riots in the East End of London when shops whose owners had German names were looted and gutted. The Press ran a campaign against Germans, and the *Daily Mail* encouraged its readers to ferret out German sympathisers or anyone with a German connection:

REFUSE TO BE SERVED BY AN AUSTRIAN
OR GERMAN WAITER.
IF YOUR WAITER SAYS HE IS SWISS
ASK TO SEE HIS PASSPORT.

Air raids and naval bombardments

The dislike and suspicion felt for enemy aliens in Britain were intensified during the early months of the War when the Germans launched naval and air attacks against Britain itself. On 16 December 1914, a German cruiser force shelled Hartlepool, Whitby and Scarborough on the East Coast, and some 137 people were killed. Air raids by aero-

planes or Zeppelins (airships) were launched against targets on the east coast and London. These raids did not cause many casualties, but they brought home to the civilian population that this was a war involving everyone in some way or another. The raids also brought a rash of scare stories about German spies, and anyone flashing a light or loitering around a dockyard or military establishment was likely to be reported and arrested.

Social life

Not only did the War bring shortages, regulations and air raids, but it also produced changes in the whole social life of the British people. With the increased wages to be earned in war work, there was more money available for entertainment, and soon there was a marked increase in the numbers attending restaurants and bars, music halls, the theatre and the cinema. Cinemas had been established in many towns and cities before 1914, but previously they had not been very highly regarded. Now with the outbreak of the War they became the main entertainment for millions of people, and stars like Charlie Chaplin became immensely popular:

> 'There are a good many picture palaces in the district (East End of London); they are very well attended and the level of behaviour maintained is good. The audiences comprise many mothers with their children – not so many fathers since the war but many soldiers on leave and others who have been wounded attend there. The factory lads and lasses attend in great numbers. I consider the entertainments are a great improvement on the old penny gaff, the old music-hall and club entertainments, particuarly in view of the fact that no drinking is permitted.'

Many public figures became alarmed at the supposed dangers to morals from the new cinema palaces, however, and tales were spread of indecent behaviour occurring in the darkness of the cinema. Some cinemas appointed wardens to patrol the rows and seats, but a later investigation found that the charges had been exaggerated:

> 'Mr F.R. Goodwin, representing the Exhibitors of London, asserted that in many cases the charge should never have been made. "When investigation is made it is usually found that the alleged misconduct is nothing more than the privileged manifestation of affection between the sexes. Most unmarried couples sitting in close proximity at entertainments will hold hands, or link arms, or even an occasional arm will be found round a waist, this under the strongest as well as under the very much diminished lighting."'

Liquor legislation

Throughout the War, however, there also existed a general feeling in Britain that somehow it was wrong for people to be enjoying themselves too much while the soldiers were fighting and dying. Criticisms were made of hostesses who organised lavish supper-dances, and newspapers denounced all-night parties where rich foods and drinks were consumed and wasted. In particular there was widespread alarm at the heavy drinking that was now taking place amongst all sections of the community. Stories were told of workers being unable to perform their duties through excessive drinking, and claims were made that production in the shipyards, steel works and munitions factories were being seriously affected. Demands were, therefore, made that the government should step in to control the selling of drink so that such evils and abuses would be ended.

Up to 1914 all premises in Britain selling alcohol had to obtain a licence from the local authorities, but this did not seriously limit the amount of drinking. In Scotland licensed premises might be closed by 9.0 p.m., but in London and other English cities they could remain open till midnight. Workers and others could drink right through the day, and it was this practice that was now being criticised. The King tried to help the situation by declaring on 15 April 1915, that he was 'taking the pledge', but since few people followed his example, the government felt it must take more direct action. Initially powers were given to naval or military authorities to limit the hours of licensed premises in the neighbourhood of any defence establishment, and then it established a Central Control Board (Liquor Traffic) with powers to regulate liquor licences in areas where excessive drinking might affect the war effort. Hours were strictly limited, and a ban was imposed on the custom of 'treating'. In 1916 the government went even further and the State itself took over the ownership of licensed premises in three areas: Enfield Lock in London, the Borders area round Carlisle, and Invergordon in Scotland.

Other measures taken to control drinking were the raising of the price and the altering of the strength of spirits and beer. Seventy degree proof was laid down as the maximum for spirits, while the strength of beer was reduced. Many workers resented the new 'weak beer', and spoke darkly of resistance and revolution, but there can be no doubt that all the regulations brought about a very considerable change in the drinking habits of the British people. Convictions for drunkenness fell sharply, while grocers were reporting that much more money was being spent on foodstuffs:

> 'The extent of the fall in public drunkennesss may be judged broadly from the fact that in 1914 the total number of convictions in Greater London and the cities and boroughs in Great Britain with a population of over a hundred thousand, was approximately 156,000, and in 1916 was reduced to 77,000, the corresponding figures for women being 41,000 and 14,000 respectively. Increased efficiency and improved time-keeping have resulted, with a consequent material increase in the industrial output.'

DELIVERING THE GOODS.
In 1915 Lloyd George became the Minister of Munitions

Summer time

Another action of the Government which affected the lives of the British people was the introduction of summer time in May 1916. This was designed to provide more daylight working hours for war production during the summer months, but there was some opposition to this development, particuarly among farmers and agricultural workers. Some farmers refused to alter their clocks, and this caused difficulties in those households where the fathers were keeping to the old time and the children were compelled to follow summer time in their schools.

Munitions Act

The government measures concerning drinking and summer time certainly influenced the life of the nation, but much more important was the control it came to exercise over industry in those war-time years. On 4 August 1914, it took over control of the railways, for as in all the European countries, the railways were absolutely vital for the transport of its troops and its munitions. Over a period it also took over the country's shipping, and it became responsible for the purchase of essential goods from abroad. It was vital, too, that a steady supply of munitions should be maintained, and from

November, 1914, the Admiralty and War Council had special powers to move into armaments factories to secure full production. In May 1915 a Munitions of War Act was passed giving the government powers to take over direct control of factories engaged in war production. A Ministry of Munitions was set up with powers to establish National Factories under its direct control, and by the end of July, 1915, there were 16 such factories.

Trade unions

The Munitions Act also gave the government considerable powers over the workers. Right from the beginning of the War the trade union leaders had shown themselves ready to cooperate with the government, and agreements had been made in the engineering industry permitting the employment of women and dilutees (semi-skilled workers) in munitions work. In March 1915 the union leaders agreed that workers engaged in war work should give up the right to strike and that disputes and wage rates should be settled by arbitration. The agreements were included in the Munitions Act, but the government went further by declaring that no employer could take on a workman who had within the previous six weeks been employed in munitions work.

Shop steward movement

It soon became clear, however, that some of the ordinary workers in Britain disliked the agreements that their leaders had made with the government to help the war effort. First signs of dissent appeared on Clydeside towards the end of 1914 and the beginning of 1915. In February 1915 some five thousand engineers in Glasgow went on strike over a wage claim, and organising this strike was a committee of shop stewards from a number of engineering shops. Previously the shop steward had been a rather unimportant local official, but he now moved forward to provide the leadership that had been abandoned by the trade union officers. The strike ended when the men accepted a penny an hour increase, but the shop stewards formed themselves into a Clyde Workers Committee to oppose the agreement made by the union leaders in the Munitions Act. They were particularly concerned about dilution, and they also came to oppose violently the rises in housing rents that were taking place. Several of the leaders were arrested, but the shop steward movement flourished to remain an important element in trade unionism.

Industrial troubles also broke out in the South Wales coalfield, and here a body of local officials, the Unofficial Reform Committee (South Wales Miners), emerged to lead a strike in July 1915 over national wage agreements. The government attempted to make use of the provisions of the Munitions Act, but this merely antagonised the miners. Lloyd George, the Minister of Munitions, was forced to visit Wales, and the Government agreed that the miners' wages should be increased.

Politics

The events of the early months of the War had also a considerable effect on British politics. In 1914 the Liberal Government had a substantial majority under the Prime Minister, H.H. Asquith, but many of its leaders still believed in the old Liberal doctrines of freedom and individualism, and they were not enthusiastic about the moves towards increased government control of the war effort and the national life. This attitude, together with reports of a growing shell shortage in France, brought mounting criticisms, and in May 1915 this led to the setting up of a Coalition Government under Asquith which included Conservative and Labour

Asquith (front left) with his war-time cabinet

Ministers. Lloyd George, the most energetic and determined of the Liberal leaders, became Minister of Munitions to deal with the shell crisis. Bonar Law, the Conservative leader, became Colonial Secretary, and Arthur Henderson, the Secretary of the Labour Party, became President of the Board of Education and a member of the Cabinet. Thus the needs of war had brought the Labour leaders, together with the trade union leaders, into the centres of government power in Britain.

Exercises   Chapter Six

1 a) Explain how the War affected the position of the following in Britain:
  i)   The Trade Unions
  ii) Enemy Aliens   6
b) Discuss why and with what consequences the Government introduced the following measures:
  i)   The Defence of the Realm Act (D.O.R.A.)
  ii) The Munitions Act
  iii) Liquor Legislation   9

c) Show how a Coalition Government came to be set up in 1915.   5
                                                          (20)

2 The following is an extract from a description of the impact of the War on London.
'From the crowd which throngs the earlier trains to London, between 7 o'clock and 9, only perhaps the station-master and the porters could tell you how many familiar faces of the younger men are missing. The regular traveller is at most aware that certain of his personal acquaintances have gone; and beyond that he has the impression that on the platforms now there are more women and fewer men than there used to be.'

a) Give examples of how the War was greeted with enthusiasm in Britain in 1914.   3
b) By what means and with what success did the Government encourage men to join the armed forces in the first two years of the War?   5
c) In what ways did women contribute to the war effort?   6
d) How did the War help to affect the social life and position of women in British society?   4
e) Illustrate and explain the attitudes of the Suffragettes towards the War.   2
                                                          (20)

3 Imagine you are a citizen of London who has been involved in an air raid. Write a letter to a friend telling of your experiences and saying how it has influenced your attitude towards the War.   (20)

4 'Our New Sisters!' Imagine you are a journalist in 1916. Write an article under the above title about the impact the War has had on the lives of British women and their position in society.   (20)

Chapter Seven

The titanic struggles

The Western Front

Although Germany and her allies had achieved considerable success during 1915, their leaders had come to the conclusion that they would have to inflict a complete defeat on their main enemies, Britain and France, before they could secure final victory. Accordingly they decided to make an all-out effort on the Western Front in 1916 in order to achieve decisive results there. The Allied leaders, too, were convinced by the failure of their Dardanelles campaign that the main struggle lay on the Western Front in France, and they prepared to make even greater efforts there in the coming year. The scene was set for an even greater escalation of the struggle with even mightier armies and forces being flung into the cauldron of the trenches in France.

Verdun

As the Germans prepared their plans for the struggle in France in 1916, they decided to take full advantage of the grim realities of trench warfare. There seemed little prospect of a break-through, so General Falkenhayn opted for a war of attrition where he could inflict such casualties on the French that they would be fatally weakened. To achieve this objective he decided to attack a key position in the French line which they would feel obliged to defend at all costs. The site selected was the ancient fortress of Verdun which controlled a vital route leading to Paris and which held a very special place

in French history and in the hearts of the French people as a symbol of their former greatness. Falkenhayn calculated that the French would rush in reinforcements if Verdun were threatened and that huge numbers of them could be killed there.

The Germans themselves brought up huge forces in preparation for their offensive which opened in February 1916. They attacked on a narrow front, and a massive artillery bombardment preceded the assaults. On one day alone, it has been calculated, over 100,000 gas shells rained down on the French forces. As the Germans had predicted, the French prepared to fight to the end, and they fought desperately for every inch of territory.

French soldiers within the shelter of Verdun

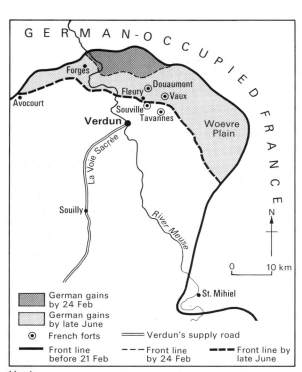

Verdun

Fierce counter-attacks were launched across the sea of mud, and everywhere were the corpses of the dead who had fallen as the struggle passed back and forward across the scarred landscape. Many deeds of heroism were performed in this nightmare struggle, and still the French held on, inspired as they were by the famous watchword of their Commander, General Petain: *Ils ne passeront pas.* – 'They shall not pass.' Thus despite all their efforts the Germans failed to seize Verdun and after five months the offensive was called off. But the French army had indeed suffered colossal losses in this epic battle, for some 315,000 of their soldiers became casualties as against 280,000 Germans.

The Somme

One of the factors that had led the Germans to reduce their attacks at Verdun was the opening of a great British and French offensive against the German lines on the Somme in the summer of 1916. The new armies raised by Kitchener's recruiting drives were now trained and ready, and many units had been brought over to France. They had a new leader in General Douglas Haig who had replaced Sir John French as Commander of the British forces in France, and he was eager to make an immediate impact. He was a firm believer in the vital importance of the Western Front, and with the powerful new forces under his command he felt he could strike a decisive blow against the enemy. He had made a close study of the battles of the previous year, and he was convinced that he could achieve the longed for break-through by employing massed forces in the attack and by destroying the enemy trenches by an artillery bombardment that was greater than anything that had gone before.

During the last week of June 1916, therefore, some 2,000 British guns laid down a ferocious five-day bombardment of the Germans lines. Then at dawn on 1 July the British armies moved in to the attack. But once again the bombardment had failed to destroy the deep German dugouts, and when the infantry attack began, the Germans emerged into the trenches to pour a withering rifle and machine-gun fire on the attackers. Terrible casualties were inflicted on the advancing British soldiers, and on the first day of the attack some 20,000 were killed, and 40,000 wounded or taken prisoner. Here is a vivid account of the scene after one British unit had been beaten back:

'Immediately in front, and spreading left and right was clear evidence that the attack had been brutally repulsed. Hundreds of dead were strung out like wreckage washed up to a high water

73

mark. Quite as many died on the enemy wire as on the ground, like fish caught in a net. They hung there in grotesque postures. Some looked as though they were praying; they had died on their knees and the wire had prevented their fall. It was clear that there were no gaps in the wire at the time of the attack. The Germans must have been reinforcing their wire for months. It was so dense that daylight could barely be seen through it. Who told the planners that artillery fire would pound such wire to pieces, making it possible to get through? Any Tommy could have told them that shell fire lifts wire up and drops it down, often in a worse tangle than before.'

Despite these appalling losses, the generals rushed up more reinforcements to carry on the offensive. For week after week, and month after month, assaults were launched against the German lines, but although the enemy was pushed back a few miles here and there, no break-through was achieved. During the battle the British first used tanks, but only a small number were engaged and they had only a limited effect. At length after five weary and bloody months the offensive was called off at the end of November. Once again fearful losses were incurred, with some 418,000 British troops, 194,000 French and 650,000 Germans becoming casualties in this terrible battle.

The fearful casualties suffered by both sides in the titanic struggles of 1916 caused dismay and alarm among the staffs at the headquarters of the various armies. They had gathered together their

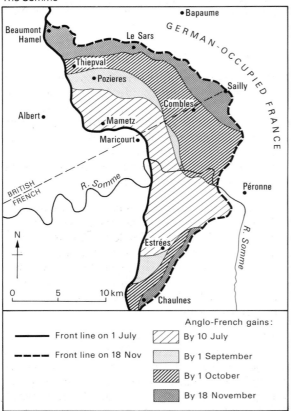

The Somme

Canadian troops fix bayonets before going 'over the top'

The Kaiser with Hindenburg (left/and Ludendorff (right))

Haig at British Army Headquarters

mighty forces for a great attack that they believed would bring victory, but now their hopes and ambitions had all petered out into a continuing stalemate on the Western Front. Throughout the year the British and French had suffered 1,200,000 casualties, while the Germans lost 800,000 men. Falkenhayn was replaced as Supreme Commander of the German forces by General Hindenburg (with General Ludendorff as his second-in-command), for his plan to exhaust the French by a war of attrition had brought such casualties to the Germans themselves that Ludendorff was later to claim that the German Army had been 'completely exhausted by the battles on the Western Front in 1916'. France, too, suffered from her tremendous exertions, and her losses were to have serious effects on her army the following year. General Haig, the British Commander, received certain criticisms for the failure of the Somme offensive, but the year had certainly marked the advance of Britain to the ranks of the great military powers. The German High Command had been astonished to see her put such a large and effective army into the field, and henceforth Britain was to play an ever larger part in the land battles of the war.

War in the air

1915 had ended with the British using their DH2s in an attempt to win air supremacy back from the Germans. They also began to fly in formations of from three to six planes, for the fighter flying on its own proved very vulnerable. Now there were fierce dogfights as the Germans, too, began flying in formations or 'circuses', and the pilots had to learn a new pattern of aerial warfare:

'The basic air battle was begun by diving at the enemy out of the sun, getting on his tail if possible, and shooting him down. If that failed to inflict a mortal wound as one passed him by, then one would try to climb again and blast him with bursts of gunfire from below as one rose. If this too failed the battle could result in an ever-tightening circling.'

After some fierce fighting the Allies gained the upper hand in the summer of 1916, but when the Germans introduced a new improved plane in the Albatross D1 which carried two machine-guns, they won back control of the air. They inflicted heavy casualties on the Allied squadrons, and by the end of 1916 the average life of an R.F.C. pilot at the front was three weeks. They were horribly vulnerable in their flimsy craft, for all it required was a bullet to fracture an oil pipe and blazing petrol would turn their plane into an inferno. Pilots carried no parachutes, and thus if their plane was shot down, they went down along with it. Yet some pilots were able to survive all these hazards, and as their tally of enemy planes shot down mounted, they were recognised as air aces. One of the most famous of these was to be the German Manfred Von Richthofen, and he shot down his first Allied plane in April 1916. By the end of the year his scarlet red plane and his squadron or circus were known all over the battlefield, and he was given the nickname of the 'Red Baron'.

The 'Red Baron'

Throughout 1916, too, the other uses of aircraft were steadily enlarged and expanded. Planes assisted the Royal Navy by keeping a look-out for enemy shipping, while British bombers extended their raids against strategic targets behind the enemy lines. The Germans continued to send Zeppelins on raids against England, but although they caused some damage and casualties, they were not

A Zeppelin

really very effective. The German losses were often heavy: thus out of a fleet of eleven airships that attacked eastern England in October 1916, four were destroyed by gales, and most of the remainder crashed or were brought down by anti-aircraft fire.

Italy

In Italy during 1916 there was little real success for either the Austrians or the Italians as they struggled and fought across their mountainous frontier.

A military outpost in the Alps

There they experienced some of the most difficult conditions of all the war fronts, and King Victor Emmanuel III of Italy spoke feelingly of his men '9,000 feet up in the clouds for seven months, in deep snow, so close to the Austrians that at some points the men can see their enemies' eyes through the observation holes'. The Italians were faced with the grim problem of dragging their guns and supplies up the mountain slopes while all the time the Austrians controlled the high mountain passes above them. High in the mountains special Alpine units fought against the Austrians across glaciers and snow-packed slopes, and many brave men perished in gale, storm or avalanche as well as at the hands of the enemy. In such grim conditions the Italians lauched an offensive early in the year, but they made little ground and incurred heavy casualties. In May the Austrians attacked and drove a five mile wedge into the Italian lines, but an Italian counter-attack in June drove them back to their original positions. Further battles continued throughout the year, but these failed to break the deadlock on this front. The Italians were bitterly disappointed by their lack of success, and their government fell from office.

The Eastern Front

The concentration of German forces in the West during 1916 gave the Russians the opportunity to take the initiative in the East. Although they had suffered staggering losses in 1915, the huge population of Russia allowed them to bring forward new reserves and new armies. In March they launched an ill-prepared offensive against the Germans in the north in order to help the French at Verdun, but the German artillery and machine-gun fire halted the advance after inflicting almost 100,000 casualties on the Russians. Then in June the Russian General Brusilov attacked the Austrians near the Dniester River. The Austrian front collapsed and many of their Slav soldiers began deserting, and by June the Russians had advanced through Galicia to the Carpathian Mountains. The Germans now rushed reinforcements from other sectors of the Eastern Front and from France, and these helped to halt the Russian advance. The Russians continued to throw themselves against the stiffened defences, but by the autumn the offensive had ground to a halt. The battle had inflicted over 600,000 casualties on the Austrians, and it struck a fatal blow at the Austrian Empire from which it never really recovered. But the Russians had won their victory at a terrible cost, for with over one million casualties the morale of their army and civilian population received a shattering blow.

The Balkans

In the Balkans the partial success of the Brusilov offensive brought a further addition to the Allied cause. Romania had been bound by treaty to Austria and Germany before 1914, but like Italy she had refused to enter the war on their side. Now she was tempted to join the Allies, and with the hope of making territorial gains she declared war on Austria in August. The Romanians advanced across the Carpathians into Transylvania in Hungary, but their drive was soon halted. Then a combined force of Germans, Austrians, Turks and Bulgars attacked Romania along the Danube. Another army attacked from Transylvania, and soon the Romanians were caught in a giant pincer movement. By the end of the year most of Romania had been overrun, and her valuable resources of wheat and oil had fallen to the Germans.

Elsewhere in the Balkans the Allied force in Salonika had been enlarged during 1916, and in August it moved northwards to give assistance to

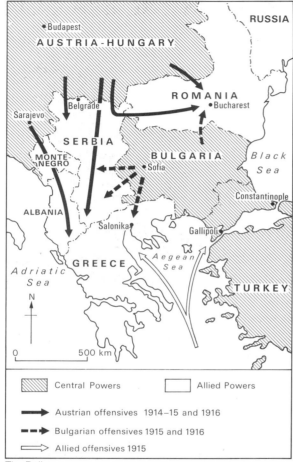

The Balkans

suffered some 50,000 casualties and the Central Powers 60,000.

Out of these various battles and operations in the Balkans, however, the Central Powers had now achieved effective control of the area. They had firm links between their home territories and their ally Turkey, and their enemies had been driven out to the extremities of the region, to the line held by Russia and to the small Allied outpost at Salonika. These successes were of considerable benefit to Germany and improved her lines of communication to all the war fronts. In addition, the granaries of Romania and other territories did something to counteract the effects of the blockade that the Allies were imposing on the Central Powers. The German victories also had the effect of isolating Russia even more from the Western Allies, and the difficulties and shortages of supply there increased the strains and tensions that were weakening the great Empire of Russia.

War at sea

Yet despite the improvement in supplies from Romania and the Balkans, the Allied blockade was indeed having more and more effect on Germany. It was being applied with increasing rigour, and Germany was experiencing shortages of food supplies and raw materials as her trade with overseas countries and particularly America was cut off. By contrast, British and Allied merchant ships were able to ply their trade throughout the world, and large quantities of food, raw materials and munitions were brought across the Atlantic from the United States. German submarines were still active against British and Allied shipping, but the danger diminished after the Germans ended their unrestricted submarine campaign because of the hostility aroused in America and other neutral countries. The U-boat was still a great menace to the Allied

the Romanians. It managed to advance about twenty-five miles against the Bulgarians, but a German force arrived to support the Bulgarians and the advance was halted. By the winter the operations had died down, and nothing had really been gained by either side save that the Allies had

GROWING TOLL OF ENEMY LOSSES IN THE SEA BATTLE

Majority of the German Light Cruisers and Destroyers Reported Lost.

FLOTILLA DRIVEN INTO THEIR OWN MINEFIELD

How Airships and Airmen Scouts Helped the German Fleet—20 Torpedo Boats Gone.

THREE ZEPPELINS BROUGHT DOWN.

Only two brief official communiqués on the North Sea battle were issued last night. Neither adds anything further to the details of the fight.

One corrects German lies about our losses and the other gives a brief summary of our casualties among officers. Admiral Beatty is reported to be unharmed.

A dramatic statement last night was that the German destroyer and light cruiser flotilla were driven into their own minefield and the majority of them lost. German survivors speak of at least twenty torpedo craft as among their "colossal" losses.

The outstanding fact is that the German Fleet—"the whole German fleet"—emerged from its Canal on "an enterprise directed towards the North." It failed in its purpose; and when the British "main forces" appeared on the scene, fled back to its base.

Yesterday three Zeppelins were reported destroyed in the battle—two shot down over the sea and one wrecked just as she got back to Germany.

Jutland. A newspaper report and the destruction of the *Queen Mary*

cause, but it had not yet reached its full potential.

The main theatre of the war at sea still continued to be the North Sea. Britain maintained her ceaseless patrols in the Straits of Dover and in the northern passage between Norway and the Orkney Islands, and continuously she convoyed troops and supplies to the armies in France. All the time the great British and German battle fleets in their bases were watching each other's every movement, ready to seize any opportunity to win a victory that might tip the naval balance and affect the whole course of the war. Always, too, the British admirals were conscious of the fact that they had the safety and security of Britain in their hands, for if they made a mistake and suffered a defeat, then Britain would be at the mercy of the Germans. As Churchill said of the Commander of the Grand Fleet, Admiral

Jellicoe, he was the only 'man who could lose the war in an afternoon'.

Jutland

And then in May 1916 there occurred the great and long-awaited clash between the two giant fleets. Admiral von Scheer had taken over the command of the German High Seas Fleet, and he determined that his naval forces should pursue a much more active policy than hitherto. In particular he decided to make use of his High Seas Fleet to undermine and erode the Allied blockade by drawing the Grand Fleet into a trap and inflicting serious damage on it. On 31 May 1916 his fleet steamed out into the North Sea from its harbours in the Baltic and Heligoland. A battle cruiser squadron under

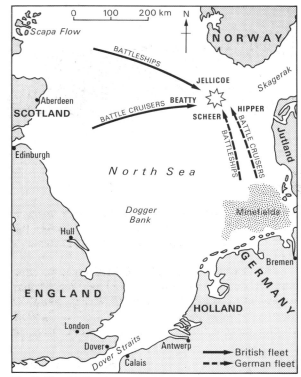

The Battle of Jutland

and in a swift encounter two of Beatty's ships, the *Indefatigable* and the *Queen Mary*, blew up and sank. The loss of the famed *Queen Mary* was a bitter blow to the British, and the manner of her going made a profound impression on all who saw it:

'All seemed to be going well with us, when suddenly I saw a salvo hit *Queen Mary* on her port side. A small cloud of what looked like coal-dust came out from where she was hit, but nothing more until several moments later, when a terrific yellow flame with a heavy and very dense mass of black smoke showed ahead, and the *Queen Mary* herself was no longer visible.'

The Germans had shown superior marksmanship during this early part of the battle, but the arrival of Jellicoe's Grand Fleet in the late afternoon swung the balance in favour of the British. The British battleships scored many direct hits on the German vessels, but the Germans now turned away for home. Jellicoe tried to intercept their retreating squadrons, but he was unable to place his fleet between the Germans and their home bases. There was a running battle for much of the night, but by morning the Germans were safe in home waters under the protection of their minefields.

A German Battle Cruiser on fire at Jutland

Admiral Hipper was sent on ahead to the Norwegian coast to tempt out the British battle cruisers, while he himself followed with the main German fleet. The plan seemed to be working when Admiral Beatty commanding the British battle cruiser squadron sailed across the North Sea to intercept Hipper. But Admiral Jellicoe had learnt of the movements of the High Seas Fleet, and he, too, set out from Scapa Flow with the British Grand Fleet.

The first action took place about 2.30 pm between the two battle cruiser squadrons a short distance off the coast of Denmark. Each was trying to draw the enemy force on to its own main fleet,

This Battle of Jutland, as it was called, did not have an immediately decisive outcome, and both sides claimed a victory. The British fleet suffered the greater damage, losing fourteen ships of some 112,000 tons as against eleven German ships of 62,000 tons. Britain, too, had heavier casualties, with more than 6,000 sailors lost in comparison with the German losses of 3,000. But though the German press hailed the battle as a great triumph, their fleet had in fact retreated to their ports, and never again during the war did it venture out to sea. It might also be said that the British with their great naval superiority could easily afford losses of ships in the ratio of fourteen to eleven. In a sense, therefore, the battle reinforced the British command of the seas, and they were able to tighten their grip round the coasts of the Central Powers. Jutland was the only major fleet battle of the War between the rival navies, and the German actions thereafter clearly left the initiative with the British Navy.

Turkey and the colonies

Meanwhile British sea-power and control of the seas continued to enable her to send troops and supplies to other battlefields and strategic areas throughout the world. The Suez Canal, for example, was a vital link in British imperial communications, and when a combined German and Turkish force had advanced across the Sinai Desert in 1915, powerful British, Australian, New Zealand and Indian forces had been poured into Egypt to meet this threat. In August 1916 a Turkish force advised by German officers again struck across the Desert for the Canal, but the British forces repulsed them after a skilful defensive battle. The British forces then began an advance across Sinai, and by the end of the year they had captured El Arish and Magdhaba. In June an Arab revolt had broken out

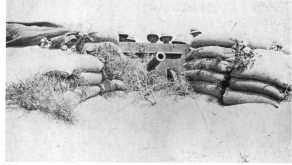

Suez Canal defences

against the Turkish overlords, and with an early success in the capture of Mecca in Arabia, this further helped to weaken the Turkish positions in the area.

Further south some 20,000 British troops commanded by the South African General Smuts began an attack on the last remaining German colony of German East Africa. They advanced on several fronts against Lettow-Vorbeck's forces, but the

The war in East Africa. A motor patrol boat is moved overland to Lake Tanganyika

German commander fought a most skilful delaying action. He received some ammunition and supplies from a German blockade runner, and this enabled him to continue the struggle. For many months he skilfully eluded the superior British forces, and frequently he outwitted their military commanders. Thus although by the end of the year the British had occupied most of the north of the country together with the seaport of Dar es Salaam, the German forces were still intact in the south of the country.

Situation

1916, therefore, had witnessed even more titanic battles than ever, and the rival armies had experienced colossal casualties that were placing great strains on their reserves and on the whole social fabric of their respective countries. And yet all the great efforts and struggles had failed to bring any decisive result, and once more the peoples of Europe had to prepare themselves for further efforts and sacrifices. For the Allies the year had been one of setbacks and disappointment, and the small victories at sea and in the colonies did not compensate them for the lack of success in France.

Exercises   Chapter Seven

1 a) Why and with what objectives did the German Admiral von Scheer decide to adopt a more active policy for the High Seas Fleet in 1916?   4

   b) Describe the naval moves and engagements that came to be known as the Battle of Jutland.   10

   c) What were the consequences of this battle for the general fortunes and conduct of the War?   6
                                                                        (20)

2 The following is an extract from a description of the British attack on the Somme in 1916.
'Immediately in front, and spreading left and right was clear evidence that the attack had been brutally repulsed. Hundreds of dead were strung out like wreckage washed up to a high water mark. Quite as many died on the enemy wire as on the ground, like fish caught in a net. . . . It was clear that there were no gaps in the wire at the time of the attack. . . . It was so dense that daylight could barely be seen through it. Who told the planners that artillery fire would pound such wire to pieces, making it possible to get through? Any Tommy could have told them that shell fire lifts wire up and drops it down, often in a worse tangle than before.'

   a) Why did the British Commander decide to attack on the Somme in 1916?   3
   b) What special preparations were made by the British forces for the offensive?   4
   c) According to the passage, what serious miscalculations had been made?   2
   d) Give a description of the opening attacks on the first day of the offensive.   4
   e) Why did the whole offensive achieve so little?   3
   f) What criticisms might be made of the general strategy adopted by the British Commanders on the Western Front?   4
                                                                        (20)

3 Imagine you are a British pilot who has been sent to a training school in Britain after serving in France between 1914–16. Write a report for the trainee pilots, telling of your own experiences, of the changes that have taken place in air warfare since the outbreak of the War, and of the dangers that the new pilots will encounter in France.   (20)

Chapter Eight

The dark days of 1917

A changing balance of power

As the countries of Europe entered their fourth year of war in 1917, it was clear that all the strain and losses were having their effects. Strikes had occurred in Austria, Germany and Britain, but within the Austrian and Russian Empires there were darker rumblings as the people protested against the grim conditions and the sacrifices demanded of them. All countries felt that they would have to make a very special effort to hold on and to win success before the strain became too great for their social structure to bear. It was to be a dark and dismal year when fateful events occurred that were to influence the outcome of the war and indeed the whole future history of the world.

1917, too, was marked by some very significant changes in the balance of forces on the two sides. Throughout the struggle both sides had been eager to gain allies and to add to their strength, and no prize could be greater than the aid of the United States. America had been traditionally an isolationist power, determined to keep clear of European affairs and conflicts, and indeed in the Presidential Election Campaign of 1916 Woodrow Wilson had successfully stood on a programme of keeping America out of the war. But from 1914 American opinion had been moving steadily against the Central Powers. The Americans had been antagonised by the German attack on Belgium, and their hostility had been increased by stories of German 'atrocities' supposedly committed in Belgium during the invasion and occupation. Perhaps the greatest factor in moulding American opinion, however, was the German campaign of unrestricted submarine warfare. The sinking of the *Lusitania* had a profound effect on American public opinion, and further incidents increased the tension. The Germans modified their policies in 1916, but their return to unrestricted sinkings early in 1917 brought matters to a head. Steadily the numbers of Americans lost in the Atlantic grew, and so, too, did the American anger. A further blow came with the discovery by the British of the 'Zimmerman telegram', a note from the German Foreign Office to their Ambassador in Mexico. This suggested that if the United States made war on Germany, then Mexico should be persuaded to declare war on the United States with the promise of recovering Texas, New Mexico and Arizona. Soon afterwards America broke off diplomatic relations with Ger-

'The Yanks are coming'

many, and on April 6 she joined the war against Germany.

The entry of the United States into the War on the side of the Allies was in part compensated for by events in Russia in 1917. As we have seen, the Russians suffered terrible losses in 1916, and these helped to produce serious riots and grave unrest in the capital and throughout Russia. In March 1917 this unrest led to revolution, and the Czar was forced to abdicate. A Provisional Government was formed which carried on the war for a period, but in October 1917 the Bolsheviks under Lenin seized power. The Germans had permitted Lenin to cross Germany to return to Russia from exile so that their enemy might be weakened, and this did indeed prove of great benefit to them. The Bolsheviks regarded the War as a capitalist conspiracy, and soon after they had seized power they withdrew from the struggle and sought to make peace with Germany.

Lenin

The Western Front

Through all these diplomatic manoeuvrings and changes, the dour struggle on the battlefields still continued. On the Western Front in 1917 the initiative tended to lie once more with the Allies. The Germans had suffered heavy losses in manpower during 1916, and now they had to spread their forces over several fronts in France, Russia and the Balkans. They decided, therefore, to strengthen their defences in the West against possible Allied attacks by constructing a heavily fortified line known as the Hindenburg Line a few miles to the rear of their existing positions. Then between February and April they made a skilful withdrawal of their troops to the new positions, leaving behind them a devastated area littered with booby traps and poisoned wells. There were strong, deep dugouts and emplacements in the new Line, and since it had been straightened and shortened it could be held by a smaller force, thereby releasing German troops for service elsewhere.

The Allies, for their part, were eager to launch new and greater offensives, for they had now a decided advantage in numbers, with four million Allied soldiers facing two and a half million Germans. The generals had recovered from the setbacks of 1916, and once again they were confident that they could win through. The first major offensive of the year was launched by the British in April at Arras, a pivot of the Hindenburg Line. The artillery bombardment was greater than ever, but although this time the Canadians captured Vimy Ridge, the overall gains were limited to a few miles. Still the casualties mounted, with the British losing 84,000 men and the Germans 75,000. Later in the month the French attacked on the Aisne with 54 divisions after an eleven-million-shell bombardment. The French commander, General Nivelle, was rash and over-confident, and boasted that he

French deserters crossing to the German side

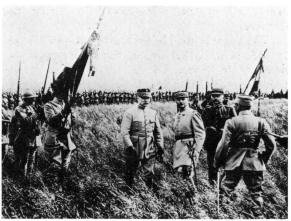

Petain (centre) on the battlefield

would win a great victory, but once again the attack was a failure. A few bulges were thrust into the German lines, but no significant gains were made. By May when the offensive ground to a halt, the French had lost over 120,000 men.

The disaster on the Aisne brought about the removal of Nivelle and his replacement by General Petain. But the defeat had even more serious consequences, for the morale of the French army was shattered and several units mutinied. The men were sickened by the seemingly futile bloodshed, and they were affected by German propaganda and by revolutionary ideas coming from Russia. A contemporary described the actions of the men and the serious nature of the crisis:

'Camps were placarded with notices declaring the intention of the soldiers to refuse to go back again to the trenches. A battalion ordered to the front dispersed in a wood. Soldiers coming home on leave sang the "Internationale" and demanded peace. Mutinies occurred in sixteen different Army Corps. A number of young

infantrymen marched through the streets of a French town, "baa-ing" like sheep to indicate they were being driven like lambs to the slaughter.'

There was a serious danger of a French collapse, but General Petain proved a wonderful source of inspiration in this hour of crisis. He visited a large number of units, and personally talked to many of the men to listen to their complaints and grievances. He sought to improve conditions, arranging for more leaves and better food. Court-martials were also set up to deal with the worst offenders, and some fifty-five ringleaders were executed. Gradually order and discipline were restored to the French army, and it was ready to continue with the fight against the Germans.

Passchendaele

In this critical situation, a heavy responsibility lay with the British army to carry on the struggle and to take the pressure off the French forces. In the

Passchendaele. The battleground (above) and stretcher bearers in the trenches

summer of 1917, therefore, the British launched a major assault against the Ypres salient with the object of breaking through and reaching the Belgian Channel ports. A preliminary attack was made against the Messines Ridge in June, and after a fierce onslaught it was seized and held. Miners had dug great tunnels out under the German lines, and the detonation of some 500 tons of explosives killed many of the defenders. The main attack began at the end of July, and this was to become one of the bloodiest and most horrible battles of the War. The German lines were pounded by gunfire, but this helped to destroy the drainage system and turned the flat, low-lying land into a quagmire after weeks of heavy rain. Thus to the normal horrors of the battlefield were added the special qualities of Passchendaele mud as the troops staggered and floundered waist high towards the enemy. The whole area became a great morass where 'men staggered wearily over duckboards. Wounded men falling headlong into the shell holes were in danger of drowning. Mules slipped from the tracks and were often drowned in the giant shell holes alongside. Guns sank till they became useless; rifles caked and

would not fire; even food was tainted with the inevitable mud.'

And yet the generals pressed on the attack for week after week and month after month. At length even they realised the futility of it all and the attacks were called off. Once more there had been no break-through, and only a few miles of territory had been gained. Once more the ground had been won at a terrible cost, with the British losing 360,000 men and the Germans 245,000. Passchendaele made a grim impression on the minds of the men who had fought there, and one British staff officer on seeing the ground after the battle exclaimed: 'Good God, did we really send men to fight in that!'

Cambrai

Some time later towards the end of November the British were more successful in another action at Cambrai when they adopted improved tactics involving the tank. Some 324 tanks and five divisions advanced in a surprise assault on a six mile front,

One of the tanks used at Cambrai (left)
Barbed wire (above)

with the troops supporting the tanks and carrying trench-bridging equipment for them. By nightfall the attack had reached the last German defence line, and a deep bulge had been thrust into the German lines. 179 tanks were lost, but they had certainly shown that they could be most effective on the battlefield. The Germans did recover most of the lost ground in a counter-attack a few days later, but for those able to grasp the full implications of the action, it was clear that a new means had been found of breaking the deadlock of trench warfare.

War in the air

Throughout 1917 the air war also intensified as the two sides pushed more and more men and planes into the struggle. The Germans had secured air supremacy by the end of 1916, but with the arrival of new machines such as the Bristol and the Sopwith Camel fighters the Allies began to reverse the tide of battle. Throughout the Spring the British pilots fought great battles with Richthofen's

circus and other German units, and in the summer the Allies launched a furious air offensive with 500 British planes and 200 French. By the end of July the Allies had once again gained control of the skies, and Allied airmen were winning fame and glory as air aces. One of the most famous of the British aces was to be Mike Mannock who first saw action over Arras in April 1917 when he shot down an observation balloon. All the time the planes were being used in close cooperation with the armies, and large numbers fought over the battlefields during the great offensives. They continued to direct the artillery fire on the enemy targets, but many planes also began machine-gunning enemy soldiers in their trenches or during attacks. Here is how one German soldier spoke of the increasing threat posed to the infantryman by air power:

'Enemy aviators keep circling around the wood we are in and signalling our presence. There is absolutely no one to drive away these parasites that give us no rest from dawn till night. Enemy aviators flying at 100 metres took part in the fighting with machine-guns. Some of our men were wounded in the head.'

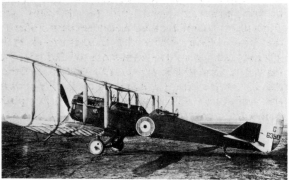

Sopwith F1 Camel fighter (top)
A D.H.9a day bomber (above)

Further developments also occurred in other aspects of aerial warfare during 1917. Thus in October 1917 the British Government established an independent air force with the task of carrying out the strategic bombing of German industry, their principal targets being railway junctions and munitions factories. The Germans continued with their bombing raids on England, but they began using Gotha bombing aircraft instead of Zeppelins. During several daylight attacks on London they caused considerable damage and casualties; in one raid in June over 600 people were killed or injured, including forty-six children killed at school.

Eastern Front

As we have seen, the terrible Russian losses and sufferings in the War had led to revolution in March 1917, and this development had serious consequences for the Russian war effort. The Provisional Government set up in March 1917 decided to continue the War, and in July the Russians launched another offensive in Galicia. They advanced about twenty miles, but when the Germans counter-attacked the Russian front collapsed and the Russian soldiers began deserting in large numbers. In a few weeks Galicia had been overrun by the Germans, while in the north their troops advanced as far as Riga. The outbreak of the October Revolution effectively ended Russian participation in the War, and the Bolsheviks sued for peace. A truce was signed in December, and a peace treaty agreed at Brest-Litovsk in March 1918. Russia lost huge stretches of territory including Poland, the Baltic provinces, areas of the Caucasus, and large parts of the Ukraine. The fighting on the Eastern Front had ended in a final victory for the Germans, and they had for a time control of large new territories.

A Russian soldier tries to stop his comrades from deserting

The Eastern Front 1916–18

The Italians retreat after Caporetto

Italy

As on the Western Front, there was bitter fighting in Italy during 1917. In the early part of the year the Italians launched further attacks against the Austrian positions, but they made only limited advances and became dispirited by their lack of success and the heavy losses they incurred. Then in October the Austrians supported by some German divisions launched an offensive at Caporetto, and here they won a resounding victory. Many Italian soldiers had lost the will to fight, and many surrendered to their enemies. All the Italian gains of the War were lost, and the Germans and Austrians pushed forward some seventy miles to the River Piave. There the Italians stood their ground, and with the assistance of British and French troops who had been rushed to the scene, the line held. The Germans and Austrians were short of troops and supplies and could not push home their advantage.

War at sea

Meanwhile the Allies were also facing new dangers and perils in the war at sea. Early in 1917 the Germans resumed unrestricted submarine warfare in an attempt to counter the effects of the Allied blockade and to strike a mortal blow at Britain's trade and lifelines. The German leaders hoped that they could bring Britain to her knees by cutting off her supplies of foodstuffs, armaments and raw materials, and they planned a fierce and determined campaign against all shipping sailing for the British Isles. Some German leaders feared that such a campaign might bring America into the War, but they calculated that they could win the War against Britain before the United States could intervene effectively.

89

Direct hit to the U-boat

minefields were laid across their sailing routes when they left their bases, while the depth charges could be thrown from destroyers to explode at depths where the U-boats might be lurking. Even more important was the introduction of the convoy system whereby merchant ships sailed in groups or convoys escorted by warships which gave protection against U-boat attacks and made it more difficult for the submarines to get at the unarmed merchantmen. By the use of all these methods, the U-boat campaign was slowly overcome, and in December the sinkings had fallen to less than 400,000 tons. Perhaps the convoy system was the most effective agent in this success, for between May and November only 11 ships of the 1,280 sailing across the Atlantic in convoy were lost.

Assistance in this desperate struggle against the U-boats also came from the United States after she entered the War in April. American warships helped to provide convoy escorts in the Atlantic, and by August 1917 there were thirty-seven American destroyers based in Europe. The entry of the United States also greatly assisted the Allies in the general struggle at sea, for the Americans had a small but efficient fleet which increased the Allied strength in several areas. The British Grand Fleet, for example, was reinforced by an American force comprising five battleships, and this further swung the balance of naval power in the North Sea against the Germans.

The German U-boat campaign of 1917 met with devastating successes. In the first three months of the year 1,300,000 tons of Allied and neutral shipping were sunk by German submarines, while in April alone more than 1Mn tons were lost. One ship in every four leaving British ports was being sunk, and there was less than a month's supply of wheat left in the country. Admiral Jellicoe confessed sadly to an American that 'It is impossible for us to go on with the war if losses like this continue'. There was a serious danger that Britain would be driven to defeat, for towards the end of April the American, Admiral Sims admitted that: 'The Allies do not now command the sea. Transport of troops and supplies is strained to the utmost and the maintenance of the armies in the field is threatened.'

Desperately the British leaders sought for a way of overcoming the U-boat menace, and gradually they began to find some answers to the problem. Rationing was introduced to conserve food supplies, while at sea the navy used minefields and depth charges to counter the U-boat threat. The

Turkey and the colonies

In the war against Turkey Britain and her allies were also to secure important successes and advantages during 1917. Steadily throughout the year British forces advanced from Sinai against Gaza and into Palestine, and by December units of the British army had entered Jerusalem. British officers like T.E. Lawrence (Lawrence of Arabia) were also

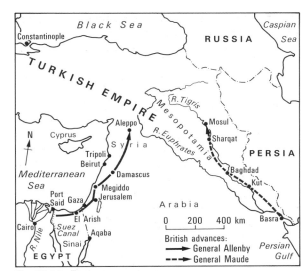
The Middle East

General Maude enters Baghdad

Lawrence of Arabia (below)

cooperating with the forces of the Arab revolt, and they engaged in raids and guerrilla attacks behind the Turkish lines and on their flanks in the deserts to the east of Palestine and Syria. In Mesopotamia the British army gained its revenge for the setbacks experienced in the early years of the War when it advanced and captured Kut and Baghdad in March 1917. The Turkish armies were reeling back from these disasters, and by the end of 1917 they were in a sorry plight. In Africa their German allies were also losing their last outposts as German East Africa was finally overrun by the Allies. One of Lettow-Vorbeck's officers surrendered here with 13,000 men, but the German commander himself managed to escape with some of his troops over the frontier into Portuguese East Africa.

Situation

1917, therefore, had been a year of grim and

terrible struggles and suffering for the many countries engaged in the War. The Allies could see certain hopeful signs with their victories in the Middle East and with their success in overcoming the worst of the U-boat challenge. Most hopeful of all perhaps was the entry of the United States into the War, for that event held out the promise of whole fresh new armies that would eventually come to the assistance of the hard-pressed Allied forces. But that day was still in the future, and for the time being the collapse of Russia into revolution and her withdrawal from the War was a most serious blow to the Allied cause. At the end of 1917 this seemed to be swinging the military balance in Europe once more to the side of the Central Powers, for it released many, many thousands of German troops from the struggles on the Eastern Front. The dark days of 1917 had been a great test for the Allies, but it was certain that equally difficult and epic conflicts and trials still lay ahead in the coming year.

Exercises   Chapter Eight

1 a) Why did the United States enter the First World War in 1917? *7*
   b) In what circumstances did Russia come to withdraw from the War in 1917? *7*
   c) How important were the entry of America and the withdrawal of Russia for the general progress and outcome of the War? *6*
   (20)

2 The following extracts are taken from comments made by Allied Admirals in 1917 about the submarine menace.
Admiral Jellicoe (Britain): *'It is impossible for us to go on with the war if losses like this continue.'*
Admiral Sims (American): *'The Allies do not now command the sea. Transport of troops and supplies is strained to the utmost and the maintenance of the armies in the field is threatened.'*
   a) With what objectives did the Germans adopt unrestricted submarine warfare in 1917? *4*
   b) What successes did their campaign achieve? *4*
   c) Was there really a serious danger that it would be impossible for Britain "to go on with the war"? *4*
   d) What measures did Britain adopt to fight against the menace presented by the submarines? *5*
   e) What was the most effective of these measures? *3*
   (20)

3 Imagine you are a British war correspondent with the Russian forces on the Eastern Front towards the end of 1917. Write a report telling of the situation there and of the dangers for the Allies presented by the collapse of Russian resistance to the Germans. *(20)*

4 Imagine you are a British war correspondent who has witnessed the British tank attack at Cambrai in 1917. Write a report describing the action and assessing the significance of this new form of warfare. *(20)*

Chapter Nine

A new Britain at war 1916–18

A changing society

The War had made a dramatic impact on the life of Britain during the first two years of the struggle, but by 1916 the pressures of the great conflict became even more intense. The epic battles of 1916 with their horrifying losses and casualties bit deeply into the national consciousness, and a grim mood of realism and determination gripped the country. More and more there was a feeling that the nation must mobilise all its resources to win the War, and people were ready to accept profound changes to

Conscripts line up for enlistment

secure final victory. In a sense the War was bringing about a significant revolution in the attitudes of the British people and in the whole structure of society.

Conscription

One of the first signs of the new mood was the introduction of conscription in 1916. A move towards conscription had appeared with the Derby Scheme of 1915 which required men to register in their various age groups, but since it did not make service compulsory, it was felt that many men were escaping or dodging their duty. A Military Service Bill was therefore passed in January 1916 giving the government powers to enlist single men between 18 and 41, and then in May 1916 a Universal Conscription Act was passed making all males between 18 and 41 liable for service. Exemptions could be given to those engaged on essential war work or to those who had conscientious objections to fighting, and tribunals were established to hear appeals from men who wished to claim such exemptions.

Conscientious objectors

The main group of men coming before the Tribunals were conscientious objectors who had some sincere objection to killing their fellow men. By 1916 such men were extremely unpopular in Britain, for the millions of people whose sons, brothers and husbands were fighting and dying on the

A typical view of a conscientious objector

Western Front believed they were nothing but cowards and shirkers. The members of the Tribunals, too, were often local businessmen who adopted a patriotic and hostile attitude towards the conscientious objectors. Normally they would reject the appeal of the conscientious objector, but sometimes they were more sympathetic to the claims that certain men were necessary for maintaining production in local firms and businesses. At Brentford, for example, the tribunal excused a beer-taster, a man supplying port wine to the army, and all the brewers of the Brewery Company.

Men who had their appeals turned down were required to serve in a Non-Combatant Corps, in an ambulance brigade or in some work of national importance. Some, however, refused to take part in anything to do with the war effort, and initially such offenders were turned over to the army authorities. One man named Howard Marten has described the treatment he received in an attempt to make him obey military orders:

'We were placed in handcuffs and locked in the cells and tied up for two hours in the

afternoon. We were tied by the wrists to horizontal ropes about five feet off the ground with our arms outstretched and our feet tied together. Then we were confined to our cells for three days on "punishment diet" (four biscuits a day and water). We were also handcuffed with our hands behind us and then placed in the cells. Rats were not infrequent visitors, and one felt a strange resemblance to an animal in captivity.'

In an attempt to exert more pressure on the conscientious objectors, a group of men were sent to France as members of a Non-Combatant Corps, and those who refused to obey orders were sentenced to death. This action caused furious protests in parliament, and the government now declared that a conscientious objector who had his appeal turned down and who would not undertake suitable service or work should be imprisoned in a civilian prison. Here they were still treated with great harshness, for Lloyd George and other ministers were determined to make their 'lot a very hard one'.

Quaker members of the Ambulance corps

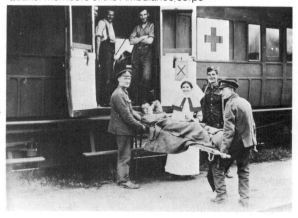

British troops man a makeshift barricade in Dublin, Easter 1916

There were about 1,500 men who defied the authorities by refusing to serve in any way, and of these some 70 died from their treatment in prison. Of the other conscientious objectors, about 3,300 served in Non-Combatant Corps, 3,000 in ambulance brigades, and 7,750 in work of national importance in Britain.

The Lloyd George Government

As the moves towards a fiercer concentration on the War intensified, there were increasing calls for a government more capable of waging total war. The government was blamed for the military reverses in France, and it was felt that a man like Lloyd George would make a more effective war leader than Asquith. Asquith had the reputation of being a cautious politician, and a famous expression of his when he had urged the House of Commons to 'wait and see' came to sum up the general feeling that he would not take decisive action to win the war.

Asquith's position was further weakened by the outbreak of rebellion in Ireland in 1916. The Irish Nationalists were bitterly disappointed by the postponement of the Home Rule Bill on the outbreak of war, and soon they were plotting military action. At Easter 1916, they seized some prominent buildings in Dublin, including the Post Office, and there was some bitter fighting before British troops could

The General Post Office, Dublin

regain control of the city. Several of the leaders of the rebellion were executed, and their deaths aroused such bitterness in Ireland that they were to bring about further troubles for the British Government after the War ended in 1918. Many people believed at the time, however, that Lloyd George had negotiated a possible settlement with the Nationalists, and that it had been the obstinacy of Asquith that had prevented its implementation.

In December 1916 the mounting criticism of Asquith came to a head, and proposals were made that Lloyd George should be given greater powers in the Cabinet. Asquith resented this proposal, and on 5 December he resigned. He perhaps thought he would be asked back into office, but now the Conservatives, together with the Labour Party and large sections of the Liberal Party swung round to give their support to Lloyd George. He was asked by the King on 7 December to form a Ministry, and soon he had formed a Government with Liberals, Conservatives and Labour members determined to spare no effort in winning the War. The *Manchester Guardian* underlined the significance of the change of Government when it declared that the Lloyd George Administration would be ready 'to take over any industry vital to the War or to the food of the people'. It also spoke of 'a mobilisation of our national resources' which would be 'decisive in its effects on the war'.

Mining industry

The new Government did indeed adopt a much more positive attitude towards the conduct of the War, and it soon gave an impetus to the movement towards greater government control of industry and the economy. It took over control of the country's coal industry, for example, for it was clear that coal supplies were a vital element in the war effort of Britain and her allies. The South Wales coalfield had been brought under government supervision in 1915, but early in 1917 the whole industry throughout the United Kingdom came under state control. A special department under a Coal Controller was set up at the Board of Trade, and an agreed rate of profits was to be paid to the former owners. The move was a highly successful one, and the Government was able to secure a more efficient and equitable supply for consumers and the munitions industries.

Lloyd George visits the front

War-time miners return to work after a strike settlement

Food supplies

The Government was also called upon to take firm action to secure adequate food supplies for the population of Britain. Some articles had been in short supply from the early months of the War, but the increasing activities of the U-boats and the unrestricted submarine campaign of early 1917 produced a real crisis. In the spring of 1917 there were only about six weeks supplies of grain in Britain, and although the immediate danger was overcome (see p.90), increasing shortages occurred throughout 1917. In London, for example, sugar, tea, butter, margarine, lard, dripping, milk, bacon, pork, condensed milk, rice, currants, and raisins were in short supply, and people had to wait long hours in queues if they hoped to make a purchase. In December 1917, *The Times* reported that:

'The food queues continue to grow. Outside the dairy shops of certain multiple firms in some parts of London women begin to line up for margarine as early as 5 o'clock on Saturday morning, some with infants in their arms, and others with children at their skirts. Over a thousand people waited for margarine at a shop

We risk our lives to bring you food. It's up to you not to waste it.

'A Message from our Seamen'

A food economy poster

in New Broad Street in the heart of the city, and in Walworth Road in the south-eastern side of London the queue was estimated to number about 3,000. Two hours later 1,000 of these were sent away unsupplied.'

Farming policies

In an attempt to ease the situation and to increase food supplies, the Government adopted a much more active agricultural policy from the beginning of 1917. In 1916 County War Agricultural Committees had been created, and these were now used to direct the work and activities of the farms. Farmers, for example, were instructed to grow more wheat and potatoes, for such crops produce more food and nourishment from a given area of land.

A food queue

The Women's Land Army in action

Before the War the free entry of foreign foodstuffs had almost ruined British farming and had caused many acres to be turned over to pasture, but now these grasslands were ploughed up. Guaranteed prices for wheat and potatoes were also introduced, while the shortage of workers on the farms was dealt with by the raising of a Women's Land Army and the recruitment of schoolboys and other volunteers. By 1918 the production of wheat was 54 per cent higher than in 1916, barley 17 per cent, oats 38 per cent and potatoes 68 per cent higher. In this way the farmers and their helpers played a vital part in the war effort, and helped to replace the food supplies from abroad lost through the action of enemy submarines.

Rationing

As well as devising policies to secure increased supplies of food, the Government had to ensure that what was available was distributed fairly. The shortages had not been affecting the community evenly, for those who could afford to pay inflated prices could always find something tasty. Rich people could also eat out in restaurants, and for a time there were special and expensive dances put on in London where the wealthy could have as much food and delicacies as they could eat. Here is how *The Times* described and denounced one such function:

'At a dance of this kind recently in a London gallery, an unlimited supply of champagne was provided. There was a smart supper set at a bar off the dancing hall, and underneath the hall was a set supper with many small tables. The menu would compare favourably with any of pre-war days. There were oysters for each of the hundreds of guests, and salmon and lobster mayonnaise. Fowl, quail, pheasant and other game were to be had in unfailing supplies. The proceedings, which began at 9.30 p.m. and continued without a break until after 5 a.m., were marked as the night wore on by scenes of the most disgusting kind.'

Initially the Government sought to deal with the situation by persuasion. In February 1917 Lord Devonport, who had been appointed Food Controller, drew up a scheme for voluntary rationing whereby every citizen was to restrict himself to four pounds of bread, 2 pounds of meat and ¾ of a pound of sugar a week. The King issued an appeal for savings in bread and flour in May 1917, but all this had little affect and did not solve the problem. In effect such proposals would have hit the poorer people harder, for they relied on bread much more than the wealthier classes.

Towards the end of 1917, the Government adopted much more severe measures. Price controls were introduced to keep the basic food items at a level where the people could afford to buy them, while subsidies were introduced for the production of flour and potatoes. Regulations were passed to prevent waste, including the using of sugar for luxury chocolates, the feeding of stray dogs, or the throwing of rice at weddings. Penalties were imposed on individuals who broke the regulations, and one unfortunate man who disliked his wife's cooking so much that he threw his dinner into the fire was fined ten pounds.

Early in 1918 the Government began to move towards a system of food rationing. In February it imposed meat rationing in London, and in April this was extended to the whole country. Rationing of tea and butter soon followed, and thus the available supplies were distributed in a much fairer way. Once the system had been introduced, it was accepted with little opposition. The Government did indeed take powers to prosecute individuals who sought to evade the rationing regulations, but in general the public supported the system wholeheartedly.

Class structure

The introduction of food rationing was one indication that a new note of fairness and understanding between the social classes was appearing in war-time Britain. In 1914, as we saw in Chapter 2, Britain was a society where there were marked differences between rich and poor and between the

A ration card

classes, but the experiences of the War had helped to bring them closer together. People from all groups had been ready to make sacrifices in the common struggle, and all had suffered the loss of friends and relations. The country was still indeed one where there were marked distinctions and differences, but the old divisions and bitterness had been somewhat blurred.

The soldiers at the front had also experienced the same coming together of the classes, for officers and men had been forced to share the same trenches and dug-outs. Men who before the War would

À LA CARTE.

Working Man. "WHAT'S YOUR FANCY, MATE? MINE'S A COUPLE O' SAUSAGES."
Peer of the Realm. "WELL, SIR, I WAS WONDERING HOW MUCH SADDLE OF MUTTON I CAN GET FOR FIVEPENCE."

The new 'equality'

never have met each other and would have known little of each other's lives and problems were now joined together in a life and death struggle. Officers and men often came to have a new respect for each other as their real qualities shone through in the grimmest of circumstances, and all this helped to overcome the gulfs and barriers that divided them.

Soldiers and the Home Front

In many ways, moreover, the soldiers felt much more separated from the civilians at home than they did from their upper class officers. Soldiers return-ing to Britain on leave did indeed enjoy all the entertainments available in London or the other towns and cities, but they often found it strange that many people at home still seemed to be living ordinary and normal lives. They also found it strange to find some civilians still talking enthusias-tically of the War and hatred for the Germans when they were quite stunned and overwhelmed by the horror of the trenches. This clash between the viewpoint of the soldier and the civilian at home is perhaps to be seen in the following letter written by a young artist and soldier named Paul Nash in 1917:

'The rain drives on, the stinking mud becomes more evilly yellow, the shell holes fill up with green-white water, the roads and tracks are covered in inches of slime, the black dying trees ooze and sweat and the shells never cease. It is unspeakable, godless, hopeless. I am no longer an artist interested and curious, I am a messenger who will bring back word from the men who are fighting to those who want the war to go on for ever. Feeble, inarticulate, will be my message, but it will have a bitter truth, and may it burn their lousy souls.'

Disillusion

The letter from Nash was only one of the many signs in 1917 of a growing disillusion with the War, and certainly such views and descriptions in-fluenced the attitudes of the civilian population. Many people were also affected by the writings of the war poets who had themselves experienced the blood and sacrifice of the trenches and who began to question the purpose of it all. The terrible casualties which filled the newspapers through 1915, 1916 and 1917 produced real feelings of horror and revulsion, while the growing shortages

'The Void' by Paul Nash

and hardships on the Home Front showed everyone the grim realities of modern war. Air raids continued against the east coast of England, and during a raid on 13 June 1917 some 162 people were killed and 432 injured. All this led a few individuals to advocate the idea of a negotiated peace, but they obtained little support from the general public. Although many people and soldiers now found the War a grim and deadly serious business, they were still doggedly determined in a new mood of realism to see it through till the Germans were finally defeated.

Propaganda: war artists

To counter this growing disillusion, the Government stepped up its propaganda efforts. A Ministry of Information was created in March 1918, and it turned out many pamphlets and portraits to maintain support for the War. Many writers, too, were recruited to produce stories about the heroism of the Allies and the atrocities of the enemy. The Ministry of Information also devised a scheme to provide a whole collection of war paintings, and artists were taken from many of the fronts to record their impressions. Paul Nash was one of these men, and his oil painting, *Void*, is a searching analysis of what modern war can mean to the men involved.

Education

The increasing sacrifices demanded of the people of Britain, together with growing disillusionment brought about by the horrors of the War, also led the government to re-consider its war aims. In seeking to maintain the country's morale, it stressed more and more that Britain was fighting for a brave new world, and thus it sought to provide some tangible signs of this utopia. In July 1918 an Education Act was passed which proposed a substantial extension of education. The school leaving age was to be fourteen (with compulsory day continuation classes for those between fourteen and eighteen not undergoing suitable alternative instruction), and local authorities were to prepare schemes covering all forms of education for their district. The intention was to provide a complete and comprehensive system which would give all young people the opportunity to secure an education best suited to their individual capacities.

Votes for women

Another move that arose directly out of the changing attitudes brought about by the War was the granting of the vote to women. In February 1918 an Act was passed by Parliament granting the vote to all adult males and to all women over 30, and at last the rights and position of women were recognised. So important had been their contribution throughout the War that most of their former opponents had altered their opinion. Even Asquith repented, declaring in the debates that 'some of my friends may think that my eyes, which for years have been clouded by fallacies and sealed by illusions, at last have been opened to the truth'.

Conclusion

The First World War, therefore, had a profound impact on the Home Front and on British society.

A war-time classroom

One of the first women voters

The civilians at home did not in any way experience the grim realities of total war that became so horribly familiar to the front-line soldier, but in its own way the society at home was quite transformed by the War. The colossal nature of the struggle produced fundamental changes in the way the country was governed and organised, and the attitudes of the people towards many issues and problems were dramatically altered. They had nerved themselves to make any change or sacrifice to help the war effort, and in the process they began to talk of creating a new world that would justify all the blood and effort that had been expended.

Exercises   Chapter Nine

1 a) Why did the British Government feel compelled to introduce conscription in 1916?   6

  b) Explain the circumstances which led to Lloyd George becoming Prime Minister of Britain in 1916.   7

  c) What steps did the new Government take to strengthen the war effort and to 'mobilise the nation's resources'?   7

                                           (20)

2 The following is an extract from *The Times* in December 1917.
'The food queues continue to grow. Outside the dairy shops of certain multiple firms in some parts of London women begin to line up for margarine as early as 5 o'clock on Saturday morning, some with infants in their arms, and others with children at their skirts. Over a thousand people waited for margarine at a shop in New Broad Street in the heart of the city, and in Walworth Road in the south-eastern side of London the queue was estimated to number about 3,000. Two hours later 1,000 of these were sent away unsupplied.'

  a) Why did food become increasingly scarce in 1917?   3

  b) What measures did the Government take to increase the supply of food in wartime Britain?   4

  c) In what ways could wealthy people escape the consequences of the food shortages?   4

  d) Why did the government eventually decide to introduce rationing?   3

  e) What regulations were made to control the consumption and use of foodstuffs in wartime Britain?   3

  f) Did rationing help in any way to bring together the people of different classes in Britain?   3

                                           (20)

3 Imagine you are a conscientious objector who has defied the authorities and has been sent to prison. Describe your reasons for being a conscientious objector, the attitudes towards you of your neighbours and friends, your experiences before the Tribunal, and your treatment in prison.   *(20)*

4 Imagine you are a former Suffragette writing a letter to a friend after the Franchise Act of 1918 has been passed. Tell of your experiences in the pre-war campaigns and during the War, and sum up your feelings now that at last the vote for women has been secured.   *(20)*

Chapter Ten

The push for victory

The Western Front: the German offensive

With the defeat of Russia towards the end of 1917, attention was focused more than ever on the Western Front, for both sides knew that the final outcome of the war must be settled there. Early in 1918 the German leaders decided that they must make one further great effort in France; and since they were now facing a war on only one major front, they knew that the troops freed from the fighting in Russia could give them the initiative in the West. It would be some time, they calculated, before the Americans arrived in France in strength, and they began making plans to achieve victory before the Americans were able to play an important part in the fighting. Once more the German generals began to dream of a decisive battle and campaign that would bring them the triumph and victory that had eluded them in 1914.

Early in 1918, therefore, the Germans began transferring huge numbers of troops from Russia to France. They planned their offensive for the early spring, and the first target selected was the weakest point of the Allied line at the junction of the French and British armies near Amiens and the Somme. General Ludendorff hoped to drive a great wedge between the two armies and thereby achieve a break-through that could lead to victory. The Germans also planned to adopt different tactics from the usual massed frontal offensives that had become the normal pattern on the Western Front. They did indeed mass a huge army of one million

men to attack on a forty mile front, but the troops were specially trained to push ahead as rapidly as possible, infiltrating through the enemy positions and bypassing or outflanking any strong points. They still proposed using an intensive artillery barrage provided by 3,000 guns, but instead of the week-long bombardments, they planned for a short and devastating barrage that would still retain some element of surprise. During the attack the artillery would lay down a creeping barrage in front of the advancing infantry as they sought to drive swiftly through the Allied lines.

The offensive opened on 21 March. The Allies knew an attack was coming, but the sheer scale and ferocity of the onslaught took them by surprise.

The German offensive. Advancing infantry passes a supply column going back

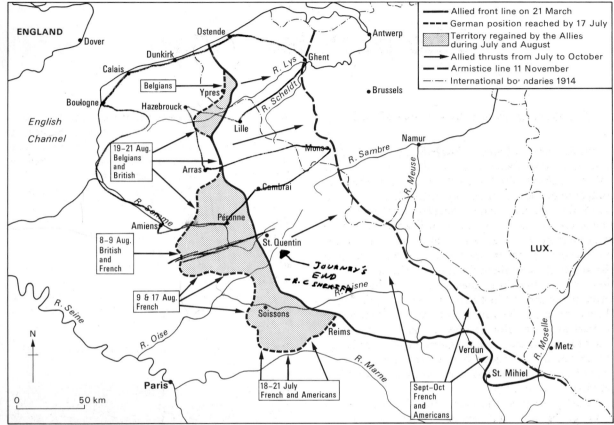

German and Allied Offensives in 1918

Many of the British artillery batteries were knocked out by gas shells, while the high explosive shells obliterated sections of the front-line trenches. The swift and massive assault of the infantry then pushed in the Allied lines on a broad front, and in four days the Germans advanced 14 miles, the greatest gain made for years in the trench warfare in France. By 24 March they were in Peronne, and the vital rail junction of Amiens was threatened. For a time it seemed that victory was in the Germans'

grasp, and it looked indeed as if the British and French armies might be prised apart. Some of the French generals suspected that the British forces might retreat away to the north to cover the Channel ports, and there was a suggestion that French reinforcements should accordingly be diverted south to defend Paris.

In this desperate situation the Allies sank many of their differences and agreed to the appointment of General Foch (later Marshal of France) as

Marshal Foch

this dire emergency, General Haig issued a famous order of the day to his troops:

'There is no other course open to us but to fight it out. Every position must be held to the last man. With our backs to the wall, and believing in the justice of our cause each one must fight on to the end.'

Desperately the Allies struggled to hold the assault as the Germans advanced over the old ground of the Ypres salient that had claimed so many British lives in all the fighting between 1915 and 1917. Seven French divisions were switched to the north, and further British reinforcements were rushed in. British aircraft joined in the fight, bombing and strafing the advancing Germans. Gradually the defenders gained the upper hand, and by the end of April the advance had been contained.

The Germans were disappointed by their failure to achieve a really decisive break-through, but they were still strong enough to launch further attacks. On 27 May they struck further south on a twenty-five mile front on the old battlefields of the Aisne,

Coordinator and later Commander in Chief of the Allied armies in France. This appointment helped smooth out some of the earlier difficulties and made it possible to guide and coordinate the activities of all the armies much more effectively. The British now threw in more reinforcements, and a determined stand managed to halt the Germans just short of Amiens. The German supply lines were becoming over-extended and this helped weaken the force of their offensive. But the Germans had won an impressive victory, with large quantities of guns and war material falling into their hands. The Allies had suffered more than 230,000 casualties and their morale had been badly shaken.

After a brief respite the Germans launched a second attack near Ypres, their objective being the railway junction of Hazebrouck and the Channel coast. The British reserves had been savaged and decimated in the earlier onslaught, and the units facing the Germans had been gravely weakened. Again the Germans made striking advances, and it seemed once more that they must break through. In

German casualties

The ruins of Ypres

This was the end of the German offensive. It had achieved considerable gains and success, coming as it did almost within sight of Paris, and failing only by the narrowest of margins from breaking through at Amiens and the Somme. The Germans had shown that the stalemate of the trenches could be broken to become a war of movement, and they had inflicted heavy losses on the Allies. Some 225,000 prisoners had been seized, while about one million Allied soldiers in all had become casualties. But the Germans, too, had suffered terribly, and they had in effect exhausted the manpower and reserves that had been transferred from Russia. They had failed to seize the ultimate prize, and now with the build up of fresh British and French reinforcements and with the arrival of American troops in France, the initiative was fast passing to the Allies. Twenty-nine American divisions had arrived by July, and the promise of an ever increasing number on the way gave new heart and determination to the Allied armies and their leaders.

'Over here'

and by the end of the first day they had crossed the river and penetrated to a depth of ten miles. By 3 June they had reached the Marne, and were now within fifty-six miles of Paris. But now the Allies were reacting more quickly, and they were able to bring in large reinforcements to hold and stabilise the line. Another German attack was launched in this sector on 9 June, but although it gained six miles it, too, was soon halted. The aggressive drive of the German troops was weakening, for they, too, had suffered heavy losses, and they were finding it difficult to supply their front line soldiers. They managed to make one final attack beginning on 15 July, however, and in a desperate assault they crossed the Marne and established bridgeheads up to four miles deep. But now the French had brought large and ample numbers of troops to the area, and they brought in great quantities of guns and ammunition. A fierce artillery barrage was laid down on the German supply lines across the river, and then the bridgeheads were assaulted in fierce counter-attacks. The Germans gave way, and soon they had all been pushed back across the Marne.

The final advance, September 1918

Allied offensives

Foch, the Allied Commander in Chief, decided that now was the time to strike back at the enemy. The first blow came in the south on July 18 when French and Allied troops attacked the salient created during the German advances. There was fierce fighting all along the perimeter of the salient, but steadily the Allied forces drove the Germans back. By early August most of the ground in the salient had been recovered, and the Germans had been pushed well back from Paris.

On August 8 the Allied attack was switched to the Amiens-Somme salient when a combined British and French force launched a determined assault. After a heavy artillery bombardment and a dawn attack by bombers of the R.A.F., an armada of 456 tanks led a great force of British, American, Canadian, Australian and French infantry against the German lines. The Germans on this occasion were unprepared and taken by surprise, and their front was rolled back. They suffered over 42,000 casualties on that first day, and some 400 guns were lost. Ludendorff later described 8 August as an especially disastrous day for the German army:

'8 August was the blackest day of the German Army in the history of the War. This was the worst experience I had to go through. Our losses reached such proportions that the Supreme Command was faced with the necessity of having to disband a series of divisions.'

From the Allied side there was an equal appreciation of the significance of this success. Here is how General Rawlinson, commander of the British Fourth Army, described the battle in his diary:

'The surprise on the 8th was complete. The Germans had no idea that the Canadians were on my front, and believed them to be at Kemmel. The tanks were all up to time, and did splendidly, and some of our armoured cars got right through the German lines and surprised the headquarters of a German corps at breakfast. We have practically eaten up seven Prussian divisions. While everyone did splendidly, I think the spirit of the Colonial infantry was probably the decisive factor. I am very proud to have commanded so magnificent an army in this historic battle.'

From now on the Allies developed a very skilful and intelligent strategy which saw them delivering a series of assaults, first on one part of the German line, and then on another. The Germans were kept entirely on the defensive, and they were unable to switch their reserves around fast enough to meet the swiftly changing and alternating blows. Steadily the Allies advanced over the old battlefields of the earlier years of the War, and the ground gained in the spring offensive was quickly recovered. The Ypres salient was abandoned, and the Germans fell back to the Hindenburg Line, but even there they could not hold back the victorious Allies. In October the British forces breached that famed defensive position, and all along the Front the Allies advanced. The stalemate of the trenches was being broken, and the Allies were winning very considerable victories after the long years of costly and fruitless offensives on the Western Front.

War in the air

During 1918 the scale of the air war in France expanded as the great German offensive and the Allied counter-offensive brought the fighting to a crescendo. The tiny air forces of 1914 had become huge air armadas, and the work and role of the air squadrons had been greatly extended. In the early part of the year the Germans had held their own in the fighting since their Fokker and Albatross machines were the equal of the British Nieuports and Sopwith Snipes, and thus they were able to give close support to their ground forces during their early offensives. But by the summer of 1918 the tide had turned decisively in the Allies' favour as their production lines poured out an increasing number of aircraft for the Western Front; and the Germans with under 2,500 planes found themselves facing about 3,500 British and 4,500 French machines. This overwhelming superiority in numbers helped

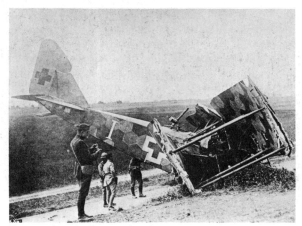
The remains of a German bomber

give the Allies air control over the battlefields, and increasingly they coordinated their operations with the military engagements on the ground. At the Marne in July, for example, Allied planes played an important part in halting the German advance, while at the Somme on 8 August some 374 planes were used to help pound the German defences. And yet although the war in the air was becoming ever more complex and more a matter of numbers, yet the skill and courage of the pilots was still an essential element in all the fighting. Losses were heavy among the squadrons of both sides, and even the greatest air ace could not hope to escape the terrible odds that faced the pilots of 1918. Both Mannock and von Richthofen were killed in 1918, the German ace being shot down in April by the British pilot of a Sopwith Camel, and Mannock being killed in July. The British ace had for some time been obsessed by a fear of being burnt alive, and to the horror of his friends his plane had burst into flames when it hit the ground after he had been shot down.

Outside the fighting above the Western Front,

there were other significant developments in air warfare in 1918. In April the Royal Flying Corps became the Royal Air force with a more independent role and position, while at sea there were significant advances that foreshadowed the future importance of air power on the oceans. In 1917 there had occurred the first successful flight of an aircraft from a ship at sea, and now in July 1918 seven Sopwith Camels took off from the deck of the aircraft carrier *Furious* to bomb Zeppelin bases on the Continent. The independent air force expanded its operations in 1918, and during the summer 500 tons of bombs were dropped on German industrial and communications targets by De Havilland day bombers and Handley-Page night bombers. In November plans were being made for a raid on Berlin from airfields in Czechoslovakia, but the Armistice intervened before it could be carried out. The German raids on England, on the other hand, steadily declined in 1918, and during their last raid on London in May seven of their Gothas were shot down. Air warfare had come of age by 1918, and already many of the most significant features of air power and strategy in the future had been tested and foreshadowed.

War at sea

1918 saw important Allied successes in other theatres, and as the year progressed news of these did much to maintain morale in the Allied countries. At sea the Allied blockade was placing an increasing stranglehold on Germany, and reports appeared of severe shortages of food and other supplies in Germany and Austria. The ability of Germany to resist was slowly being squeezed out of her, and this steady attrition of her power was beginning to affect her armies at the front. News of the food shortages at home and the sufferings of their families reached the soldiers in the line, and

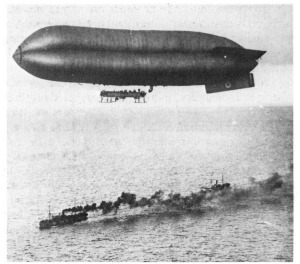

A British naval airship escorting a convoy

the fears and worries this aroused helped to undermine their morale and fighting qualities.

In the war against the U-boats, too, the Allies were achieving considerable successes. The convoy system was put more fully into operation, and steadily the submarine losses were cut down. Defences in the Channel were strengthened by the bringing in of whole new fleets of destroyers, sloops, armed trawlers and motor-boats, many carrying radio equipment that enabled them to detect submarines on the surface and, at short distances, underwater. Mines and nets were stretched across large sections of the Straits of Dover, and flare ships with their searchlights hunted out the U-boats that tried to creep out from their bases on the surface because of the risk of hitting a mine when submerged. Such were the dangers here for U-boats that many were forced to take the northern route round Scotland to reach the Atlantic, and since they thereby lost several days on the journey, their effectiveness on patrol was accordingly diminished. Steadily the Allies gained the upper hand, and with seventy-three U-boats being destroyed during the year, their menace was gradually being overcome.

A further dramatic blow was struck at the German U-boat campaign by a daring raid on their important base at Zeebrugge in Flanders in April 1918. A small naval force entered the harbour, and while marines attacked the defenders, three old warships filled with concrete were sunk across the channel leading to the submarines' moorings. The bravery of the men engaged in the raid made a deep impression on the British public, and the success of the attack did much to raise public morale and enthusiasm for the achievements of the naval forces.

The Balkans

Another Allied success was achieved in the Balkans by the army operating from Salonika now commanded by the French general, Franchet d'Esperey. This force had been largely ineffective

Zeebrugge. The British blockships in position

Salonika. British and French troops preparing for action

throughout the War, but now it made a swift advance against the tottering Bulgarian army. There was a general retreat which quickly turned into a rout, and in September 1918 the Bulgarians asked for an armistice. Bulgaria was the first of the Central Powers to leave the struggle, and her departure put more pressure on Turkey. The German control of the Balkans was loosened, and the tide of war in that area was flowing strongly in the Allies' favour.

Turkey

The resistance of Turkey, too, began to weaken and

crumble as the Allied campaign of 1918 developed. In Mesopotamia the British advanced along the Tigris to capture Sharqat and then the great oil centre of Mosul. From Palestine an advance was launched northwards against Syria, and after a victory at Megiddo, the Allies captured Damascus, Beirut, Tripoli and Aleppo. By the end of October the Turks had had enough, and they signed an armistice. Early in November an Allied fleet sailed to Constantinople, and German influence in the area was completely eliminated. The alliance of the Central Powers was fast disintegrating.

Austro-Hungary

The collapse of Turkey and Bulgaria left open the frontiers of Austro-Hungary, and that stricken Empire soon found itself in a most perilous situation. The Austrians had made a last offensive against the Italians in June 1918, but it was soon brought to a halt. Then in October the Allies mounted an offensive in Italy, and after a fierce struggle they advanced across the Piave and made considerable gains. The Austrian army lost large numbers of men through flight and desertion, and the front was in danger of collapse. This was the final blow for the Austrians, for in effect the Empire was already beginning to break up. The subject peoples of the Hapsburg Empire were demanding independence, and in the growing confusion some of them were setting up provisional governments. On 4 November the Austrians agreed to an armistice, and Germany was left on her own to face the might of the victorious Allies.

End of the War

The impact of all these reverses on Germany herself

Liberation in Czechoslovakia

German prisoners after one of the last battles

was very considerable, for she was now faced with the prospect of attacks from all quarters. At home the setbacks sapped further the morale of the civilian population, and there were growing disorders as shortages mounted. New revolutionary doctrines aroused by events in Russia were also affecting the people of Germany, and many of her leaders felt they were losing control of the situation. The army on the Western Front was increasingly affected by the growing discontent at home, and their resistance to the advances of the Allied armies weakened. There was a serious decline in the morale of the German army, and the rate of desertions increased. More and more the army commanders realised that they could not hold out much longer, and they suggested to the civilian leaders that they should ask for an armistice.

The first German approach was made at the beginning of October to President Wilson of the United States, but negotiations broke down over the conditions for a cease fire. Steadily the situation in Germany deteriorated, however, and by the end of October Ludendorff had resigned and mutinies had broken out in the High Seas Fleet. Riots and disorders spread throughout Germany, and on 9 November the Kaiser was forced to abdicate and flee to Holland. A republic was set up in Berlin, and the new government asked the Allies for an armistice. The Allies laid down conditions and insisted on the withdrawal of all German troops from occupied territories, the repatriation of all Allied prisoners, the handing over of guns, ammunition and naval units, and the evacuation of the west bank of the Rhine by all German military forces. The German delegates were shocked by these armistice terms, but the situation was so serious that the government in Berlin was forced to accept them. The Armistice came into effect at 11

Revolution in Berlin, November 1918

'So it was all over, really over! It was like the gift of another life! He would not be killed, no one else in the battalion would be killed. A thrill of almost painful exultation went through him. Then with a worse, almost unmendable pang, he thought of the millions of men of many nations who would never feel that ecstasy, who were gone for ever, rotting in desolate battlefields and graveyards all over the world.'

am on 11 November, and the Great War that had claimed so many lives had at last come to a close.

The news of the Armistice was greeted with great celebrations and rejoicings in London, Paris and other cities. But on the Western Front the reaction of the soldiers was much quieter. Many could hardly believe that it was all over, and when they finally grasped the news, they felt a deep thankfulness that they had survived:

'Thank god! The end of a frightful four years of terrible trench-assaults and shell fire; the awful winters in waterlogged trenches, cold and miserable; loss of friends, exhaustion and wounds.'

Exercises   Chapter Ten

1 a) Describe and account for the success of the Allied offensive against the Germans on the Western Front in the autumn of 1918.   7

  b) Explain the circumstances in which Germany's allies were forced to seek peace in 1918.   6

  c) Account for the German defeat in the First World War.   7

  (20)

2 The following extract is from an order of the day issued by General Haig to his troops in April 1918.

'There is no other course open to us but to fight it out. Every position must be held to the last man. With our backs to the wall, and believing in the justice of our cause each one must fight on to the end.'

  a) How serious was the crisis facing the British forces in 1918 which caused General Haig to issue this order of the day?   3

  b) Why were the Germans able to gain the initiative and to launch an offensive on the Western front early in 1918?   2

c) What new tactics and strategy did the Germans adopt during this offensive in the spring of 1918? 4

d) Give an outline of the major German attacks and their outcome. 4

e) What measures did the Allies adopt to meet the crisis produced by the German attacks? 4

f) What were the consequences for Germany of the failure of their great offensive in 1918? 3

(20)

3 'At last it is really over!' Imagine you are a British soldier on the Western Front as the Armistice comes into effect. Using this phrase as your opening words, write a letter home describing your feelings as you look back over the years of fighting and as you think of what peace will mean. (20)

4 Imagine you are a war correspondent with the R.A.F. in France in the summer of 1918. Write a report of the recent developments in the war in the air, stressing the growing power of the Allied air fleets. (20)

Tending a war grave, 1918

The Armistice

Chapter Eleven

Making the peace

The peacemakers

The ending of the War presented the Allied statesmen with an immense task. The War had brought about a colossal disruption of the old Europe, and they had to tackle the problems of restoring stability and securing a lasting peace. The Empires of Russia and Austria-Hungary had been destroyed, while in Germany the new republican government was threatened everywhere with unrest and revolution. In many places the whole social and political fabric was in ruins, and a new pattern and order of society had to be established. Immense damage had also been inflicted on the populations, industry, communications and farmlands of France, Belgium and other areas where the armies had fought, and in many countries the finances and currencies had been shattered. Millions upon millions of lives had been lost, and the flower of a generation of young Europeans lay dead or were shattered in mind or in body. The War itself, too, had aroused great hatreds and bitterness among the combatants, and this made it all the more difficult to solve the old problems that had caused the War and the new ones produced by the conflict.

Versailles

In an attempt to deal with these and all the other many problems arising out of the War, the statesmen and representatives of fifty-one Allied and Associated Powers gathered at Versailles in France in January 1919. The main figures were President Woodrow Wilson of the United States, Clemenceau, the Prime Minister of France, Lloyd George, Prime Minister of Britain, and Orlando, Prime Minister of Italy. Each of the four statesmen had distinct and different attitudes towards Germany and the general situation, and these attitudes influenced their approach to the whole process of peace-making. Clemenceau, for example, was determined that Germany should be made to pay for all the damage and losses she had inflicted on France, and he was determined to obtain real security for France against any possible German attacks in the future. Germany had invaded France in 1870 and in 1914, and Clemenceau with other Frenchmen was anxious to ensure that never again would they be called upon to face such an onslaught.

The peacemakers; Clemenceau, Wilson and Lloyd George

Peace negotiations. The Hall of Mirrors, Versailles

Lloyd George for Britain was also under considerable pressure to inflict a harsh peace on Germany. He himself had a vision of a better world where the threat of war would be removed, but British public opinion seemed vehemently in favour of making Germany pay heavily for her conduct and aggression. Lloyd George and other British leaders also saw the opportunity for seizing German colonies and for strengthening Britain's power and influence throughout the world. Orlando for Italy was also concerned to secure territories for his country at the expense of Austria, as had been promised by the Allies in 1915. Italy had suffered serious losses in the War, and Orlando was anxious that his people should feel that it had all been worth while. Unlike the other statesmen,

however, Woodrow Wilson of America did not seem quite so intent on advancing the immediate interests of his own country, and he came to Versailles with the declared aim of securing a just and lasting peace based on firm principles. In January 1918 he had announced his famous Fourteen Points which laid down important general principles about international affairs and provided solutions and settlements for the many problems of Europe and the world.

Treaty of Versailles

By the time of the Peace Conference, many of Wilson's Fourteen Points had been reluctantly accepted by the other Allied leaders, and some of

The League of Nations, Geneva

the basic principles and prosposals were incorporated in the Treaty of Versailles, the treaty and settlement which referred specifically to Germany. They agreed, for example, to his proposal in the Fourteenth Point for the establishing of a general association of nations; and thus the first articles of the Treaty of Versailles dealt with the setting up of a League of Nations, with a Council for four permanent members (Italy, Japan, France and Britain) and a General Assembly with representatives from all member states. Its purpose was stated as being to 'achieve international peace and security by the acceptance of the obligation not to resort to war and by a scrupulous respect for all treaty obligations in the dealings of organised peoples with one another'. It was also stated that no member should make war on another before the dispute had been submitted to the League. Any nation which failed to fulfil this obligation might have sanctions imposed upon it.

The European Allies, however, were not prepared to go along with all of Wilson's ideas, and they were ready to depart from the Fourteen Points in certain instances. Thus, for example, they were determined to punish Germany severely by taking additional territories from her and by exacting harsh reparations to pay for the damage she had caused. All of this was to cause major difficulties later, for the Germans claimed that they had agreed to sign the Armistice and make peace on the basis of the Fourteen Points. The European Allies did not accept this view and held that the Germans had agreed to the Armistice unconditionally.

Further difficulties and resentments were to be caused by the procedures adopted at the Conference. The Peace Treaties were in fact drawn up by the Inner Council of Four of the Allies (Wilson, Lloyd George, Clemenceau and Orlando) and then presented to the Germans for their acceptance. Thus the peace terms were not negotiated as the Germans had expected, but instead they were actually imposed on Germany by the Allies. The German envoys felt humiliated, for they had no alternative but to accept what was placed before them. Their humiliation was continued when they were brought to the famous Hall of Mirrors at the Palace of Versailles on 28 June 1919, to sign the treaty:

'Through the door at the end appear huissiers with silver chains. They march in single file. After them come four officers of France, Great Britain, America and Italy. And then, isolated and pitiable, come the two German delegates, Dr Muller and Dr Bell. The silence is terrifying. Their feet upon a strip of parquet echo hollow and duplicate. They keep their eyes fixed away from those two thousand staring eyes, fixed upon the ceiling. They are deathly pale. The one is thin and pink-eyelidded. The other is moon-faced and suffering. It is all most painful. When all had signed, "La séance est levée" rasped Clemenceau ("The session is over"). Not a word more or less. We kept our seats while the Germans were conducted like prisoners from the dock, their eyes still fixed upon some distant point of the horizon.'

Certain of the actual terms of the Treaty of Versailles also aroused considerable resentment among the Germans. They were disappointed that they were not invited to become a member of the League of Nations at this time, but they found especially objectionable the clause which allotted war guilt to Germany and blamed her for causing the War. The Germans certainly did not accept that they alone were responsible, and as we have seen (Chapter 3), the War had arisen out of a complex situation and series of crises, with all the Powers contributing some element to the tragedy. The Allies, however, were determined to affix the blame on Germany, partly in order to justify their claims for reparations. The clause was a very great affront to the Germans, and it came to colour their whole approach to the treaty. It convinced them more than ever that the Allies had broken the Armistice terms, and it was to make them more and more resentful of the treaty as the years passed.

Another clause of the Treaty did in fact provide for the payment of reparations as the European Allies had been demanding. It did not lay down the exact amounts Germany was to pay 'for the loss and damage to which the Allied and Associated governments have been subjected as a consequence of the War', but a figure of £6,600 million was mentioned. The precise figures were to be worked out at a later date, but many advisers declared that it would be impossible for Germany to pay such a sum without causing immense damage to her economy and that of other countries. Winston Churchill was one who later pointed out the dangers involved in this kind of exercise:

'The economic clauses of the Treaty were malignant and silly to an extent that made them obviously futile. Germany was condemned to pay reparations on a fabulous scale. These dictates gave expression to the anger of the victors, and to a failure of the people to understand that no defeated nation or community can ever pay tribute on a scale which would meet the cost of

French troops march into the Rhineland

modern war. Payment of reparations can only be made by services or by the physical transportation of goods, and when these goods arrive in the demanding countries, they dislocate the local industry.'

Another important section of the Treaty dealt with territorial changes that saw Germany lose approximately 26,000 square miles of territory and six and a half million of her population. In the west she was required to hand over the old disputed provinces of Alsace and Lorraine to France, the small districts of Eupen and Malmédy were given to Belgium, part of Schleswig was transferred to Denmark, and the Saar Valley, with its coalfields, was to be under the administration of the League of Nations for a period of fifteen years, after which a plebiscite would decide its future destination. In the east, parts of East and West Prussia, Posen and Silesia were handed over to the newly created state of Poland, and some of this territory went to form the Polish Corridor giving Poland access to the sea. The port of Danzig was made a free city under the administration of the League of Nations, while Memel on the Baltic was handed over to Lithuania. (Lithuania, Latvia, Estonia and Finland had been made independent of Russia by the Treaty of Brest-Litovsk, and the Allied Powers recognised their independence at Versailles.) It was agreed that after the treaty had been ratified, plebiscites would be held in Silesia, East and West Prussia, Schleswig, Eupen and Malmédy in order to define the new boundaries in accordance with the wishes of the inhabitants. Many of these changes were disliked by the Germans, and they particularly resented the creation of the Polish Corridor which cut off the German territories in East Prussia from the main part of Germany.

Germany was also called upon to surrender her overseas colonies, and these were given to one or other of the Allies under a system of mandate from the League of Nations. German South West Africa was given to the Union of South Africa, East Africa, and the Cameroons to Britain, and Togoland to France. In the Pacific the former German possessions were taken over by Australia, New Zealand and Japan. Once again the Germans criticised the terms since they regarded the mandate system as merely a thin cloak to cover the acquisition of the colonies by their victorious enemies.

A further section of the Treaty contained certain important provisions designed to keep Germany weak by limiting her military power and restricting her armaments. Her ability to strike in the west was diminished by the demilitarisation of the Rhineland, with no German troops and fortifications to be allowed on the east bank, and the west bank to be occupied by Allied soldiers for a period of 15 years. Her existing army was to be disbanded and her artillery and weapons destroyed. The bulk of her navy was to be handed over to the Allies (The High Seas Fleet had sailed to Scapa Flow, but there it was scuttled by her crews), and the fortifications at Heligoland and other places commanding the

British occupation troops in Cologne

The German Fleet on its way to Scapa Flow (above)
One of the German battleships scuttled at Scapa Flow (right)

routes between the North Sea and the Baltic were to be dismantled. In future Germany's army was to be restricted to 100,000 men, recruited as volunteers and not by conscription, while her naval forces were limited to six light battleships, six light cruisers, twelve destroyers and twelve torpedo boats. In addition she was forbidden to manufacture poison gas or to build tanks, and she was allowed no military or naval air force.

Several other economic, political and general clauses were also included in the Treaty to cover a wide range of terms and conditions. Germany was forbidden to unite with Austria, for example, and thus an attempt was made to limit any possible expansion in that direction in the future. Several of Germany's waterways were placed under interna-

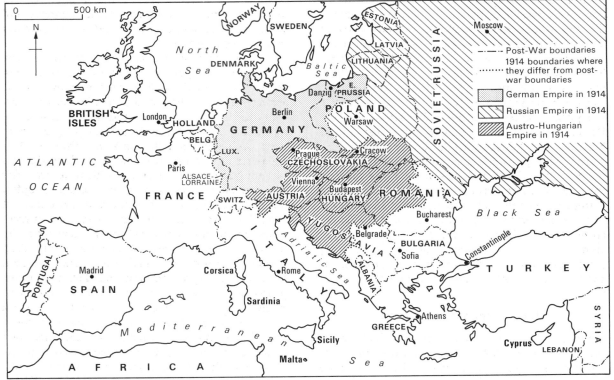

Europe after the peace settlements

tional control for a period, while the property of Germans in Allied countries was made liable to confiscation to meet any outstanding debts owed to Allied citizens. There were also clauses which provided for the trial of the ex-Kaiser and certain other Germans accused by the Allies of war crimes.

Other Treaties

To deal with the situation concerning Germany's allies, other treaties were drawn up by the delegates at Versailles, and in all of them (Austria – Treaty of St. Germain; Hungary – Treaty of Trianon; Bulgaria – Treaty of Neuilly; Turkey – Treaties of Sèvres and Lausanne), there were clauses referring to the setting up of the League of Nations. In a sense these treaties recognised what had already taken place in central and eastern Europe, namely the splitting up of the Austro-Hungarian Empire into the component parts formed by the subject peoples. Austria and Hungary were left as small land-locked states after Galicia and other territories had been transferred to Poland and the new states of Czechoslovakia and Yugoslavia had been formed. Czechoslovakia was formed out of the old Austro-Hungarian provinces of Bohemia, Moravia, Slovakia and Ruthenia, while Yugoslavia was based on the old Serbia, with the addition of such territories as Croatia, Bosnia, Herzegovina, Slovenia, Dalmatia and Montenegro, most of them from Austro-Hungary. Austria lost further territories in the Tyrol to Italy, and the Italian frontier was pushed across the disputed border lands to the Brenner Pass. In the Balkans Bulgaria lost land to Yugoslavia and Greece, while Romania made very considerable gains in Transylvania, Bessarabia and the Bukovina. Turkey defied the terms of the first treaty imposed on her, and eventually her losses in Europe were confined to a small part of Thrace. She gave up her rights in Egypt, Cyprus and the Sudan (controlled by Britain), and of her former Arab Empire, Syria, Lebanon, Palestine and Iraq (Mesopotamia) became mandates of Britain or France, and Arabia became independent.

Assessment of the Treaties

When the delegates at Versailles had finally completed their work, they had in effect brought about a massive re-shaping of the map of Europe and the old colonial areas of the world. Out of the former Austro-Hungarian, Russia and Turkish Empires had been carved a host of new countries and states, and the whole pattern of power and responsibility in these areas had been quite transformed. The simultaneous collapse of the three great Powers of Russia, Germany and Austria-Hungary had presented a unique opportunity in Central and Eastern Europe, and the peacemakers had sought to give expression to the fervent desires of the peoples of the area that they should freely rule and govern themselves. To many observers, the new Europe, based as it largely was on the principles of nationalism and self-determination, was a more just and equitable place than the old world of empires and militarism, and they confidently believed that out of all the struggles and changes could come a new and more hopeful future.

But those who looked more closely at the settlement could perhaps see that there were many serious flaws and difficulties inherent in the various arrangements. Although the creation of the new countries in Europe did indeed help to realise the aspirations of the formerly subject peoples, there were problems from the start that threatened to endanger their prosperity and survival. In the first place it had proved extremely difficult to draw fair and just boundaries between the various peoples, for old patterns of settlement and movement of peoples had resulted in a complex mixture of races in certain places. Thus each of the new countries tended to have sizeable minorities within their borders, and not surprisingly such minorities soon began expressing a wish to be joined with their own people across the border. This problem was intensified when borders were drawn up to give extra gains and special benefits to the victorious countries. Three million Germans, for example, were included in the new Czechoslovakia so that she could have the mineral resources of Bohemia and a secure frontier based on a mountain barrier. Within the new states, too, there were normally more than one major people, and this often led to strains and internal conflicts. There were serious rivalries between the Czechs and Slovaks in Czechoslovakia, for instance, while in Yugoslavia the disputes and differences between the Serbians, Croatians, Bosnians, Montenegrins and other peoples created very great difficulties for the new government.

Nor did the Treaties really provide a final settlement of all the old quarrels that had wracked Europe and the Balkans. Thus on the frontiers between Romania, Bulgaria, Greece, Yugoslavia, Poland and Czechoslovakia were tensions, rivalries

The break-up of the Turkish Empire

and suspicions, and here were all the dangers of new quarrels and conflicts. It could not be assumed, moreover, that the interests and ambitions of Russia and Germany in the Balkans could be ignored indefinitely. Both were at present weak and unable to intervene, but inevitably the day would come when they would seek to restore their influence and traditional ties with the area and its peoples. It could also be objected that the settlement in Central Europe and the Balkans had created serious economic problems for the future. Many of the new countries were too small to be entirely viable, while often the new frontiers cut sharply across trading routes and market outlets. Thus, for example, the Danube basin perhaps presented a natural economic and trading area, but the newly erected customs barriers interrupted the smooth flow of trade and commerce to the possible impoverishment of the peoples concerned. The old Austro-Hungarian Empire had perhaps been more of a natural economic unit, and the new arrangements might not be in the best economic interests of the region.

Certain other criticisms of the Treaties stressed

the failure of the peacemakers to deal with the problem of disarmament. The War had been in part caused by the great armaments race before 1914, but now only Germany and her former allies were to be disarmed. There were general discussions and proposals to hold later disarmament conferences, but in this vitally important area nothing concrete was achieved. The issue of reparations also hung over the settlement like a cloud, and it was to poison the economic and political situation in Europe throughout the 1920s. Even more serious was the fact that the United States Senate did not ratify the Treaties and the formation of the League of Nations, and she made separate agreements with her former enemies. The United States did not join the League of Nations, and thus that great hope for international cooperation and the peaceful settlement of disputes was gravely weakened at the outset.

Perhaps the greatest criticism of the Treaties, however, was their failure to deal adequately with the German problem. Germany, as we have seen, had been a giant in the old Europe before 1914, and her energetic and aggressive policies had alarmed the other Powers and had played a part in bringing about the War. The War itself had illustrated the colossal strength of Germany, for the power and resources of a huge coalition had been required to bring her to eventual defeat. To remove this German threat to the stability of Europe in the future, the Allies had perhaps two alternatives: to crush Germany and so limit her power that she would be incapable of attacking her neighbours, or to win her over to peaceful and willing cooperation with the other nations of Europe and the world. The settlement failed to adopt consistently either of these alternatives, and in a sense the Allied leaders wavered uncertainly between one and the other. Thus the military restrictions imposed on Germany were more of a punishment and an irritation than a serious attempt to curb and restrain her indefinitely, and certainly Germany would one day be recovered sufficiently to challenge and ignore them. Nor did the settlement seem a fair and honourable one that could win the cooperation of the Germans, and right from the beginning they had bitter and perhaps justified complaints. They objected to its being imposed upon them, they were antagonised by the clause which allotted them complete responsibility for the War, they resented the huge reparations bill, and they felt strongly that they had been deceived in that the settlement was not really based on the principles of the Fourteen Points as they had expected. All over Europe they saw new nations being created to satisfy the principle of self determination, but all around in the Sudetenland (Czechoslovakia), Silesia, Danzig, Memel and elsewhere Germans were being transferred to foreign rule and domination. For the moment Germany was powerless to resist the imposition of the Treaties, but one day, it seemed certain, she would seek to redress her grievances and seek to overturn many of their provisions.

Conclusion

The delegates at the Peace Conference at Versailles, therefore, had carried through a monumental task whereby they had in effect re-drawn the map of Europe. They did make a serious attempt to create the basis for a more just Continent than the old Europe that had plunged into war in 1914, and certainly in the League of Nations and in the principle of self-determination for the peoples of Europe they had sought to lay the foundations of a more equitable international order. But their failure to deal adequately with the German problem, and the difficulties and resentment caused by such features as reparations, the war guilt clause, and the placing of German minorities and territories within other countries all helped to undermine the moral and political basis of the Treaties. Increasingly during the 1920s and 1930s there was a growing antagonism to the Peace Treaties, particularly in Germany, and new German governments were to appear whose prime task it was to overthrow the Versailles Settlement. As it turned out, the Settlement was not a final solution of Europe's problems, but more a twenty years' truce before another war would convulse and devastate the Continent.

Exercises Chapter Eleven

1 a) What were the main aims of the representatives of Britain, France and the United States in drawing up the peace treaties at Versailles in 1919? *5*
   b) Outline and explain the main terms of the peace settlement with Germany. *9*
   c) Assess and criticise the work of the Peacemakers at Versailles. *6*
   (20)

2 The first extract is from Article 231 of the Treaty of Versailles and the second from a book written by Winston Churchill.
   'The Allied and Associated Governments affirm and Germany accepts the responsibility of Germany and her allies for causing all the loss and damage which the Allied and Associated Governments and their nationals have been subjected to as a consequence of the war imposed upon them by the aggression of Germany and her allies.'

   'The economic clauses of the Treaty were malignant and silly to an extent that made them obviously futile. Germany was condemned to pay reparations on a fabulous scale. These dictates gave expression . . . to a failure of the people to understand that no defeated nation . . . can ever pay tribute on a scale which would meet the cost of modern war. Payment of reparations can only be made by services or by the physical transportation of goods, and when these goods arrive in the demanding countries, they dislocate the local industry.'

   a) Why did Germany accept the above clause which declared her responsible for causing the War? *3*
   b) What was the German reaction to the clause blaming them for causing the War? *3*
   c) To what extent were the Germans in fact responsible for causing the First World War? *6*
   d) What reasons did the Allies bring forward for imposing reparation payments on Germany? *2*
   e) Discuss the dangers and difficulties that were involved in imposing reparations on Germany. *3*
   f) Why should the Germans have believed that the imposition of reparations was unjust? *3*
   (20)

3 Imagine you are a journalist present in the Hall of Mirrors at Versailles on the day the German envoys sign the Treaty of Versailles. Write a report of the scene, the atmosphere and the personalities, give an account of the treaty, and comment on the prospects of it providing a lasting peace in Europe. *(20)*

Chapter Twelve

A brave new world

Ending of the War in Britain

Although the Peace Settlement did not solve all the problems that had caused and that had been raised by the War, most people in Britain felt that with their victory in that great conflict they stood on the threshold of a brave new world. During the conflict the authorities had sought to call forth the full cooperation of the people by insisting that the War was a great crusade, a war to end all wars, and that the world they would live in after victory would be quite transformed. Thus when the Armistice was signed, it is not really surprising that the country at home burst forth in a great outpouring of joy and celebration. All over the country people expressed their joy that the killing had stopped and that the guns had been silenced. Here, for instance, is one description of the scene in London on Armistice Day, 1918:

'It seemed as if one heard a dead silence and then that the whole nation gave a sigh of relief. A few moments later the people had gone mad. They hurried into the streets. Omnibuses and taxis, vehicles of every kind were commandeered by cheering women and girls, with here and there an elderly man, young men on leave and wounded soldiers in hospital blue. The crowds cheered and sang as they flocked to Buckingham Palace. Now to add to the press came people from all over London – girls in their factory overalls and caps crowd into lorries, and as if by magic London has become a city of flags. One

sees a stout elderly Colonel on the top of a taxi beating violently a dinner gong. Presently, because the crowds are so dense, all traffic is stopped.'

Such demonstrations have frequently been criticised over the years as being rather hysterical and inappropriate outbursts, and certainly they contrasted markedly with the quiet, thoughtful and serious mood of the soldiers in France at this time (see p. 114). And in Britain, too, there were many families for whom the gladness and the rejoicing at the ending of the fighting were quite overshadowed and saddened by what the War had come to mean to them. Over 900,000 soldiers from Britain and the

Armistice day, 11 November 1918

The unveiling of the Cenotaph

'All those with whom I had really been intimate were gone; no one remained to share with me the heights and the depths of my memories. As the years went by and youth departed and remembrance grew dim, a deeper and ever deeper darkness would cover the young men who were once my contemporaries.

For the first time I realised, with all that full realization meant, how completely everything that had hitherto made up my life had vanished with Edward and Roland, with Victor and Geoffrey. The War was over; a new age was beginning; but the dead were dead and would never return.'

In such a situation it was only to be expected that some people in Britain should feel bitter about the terrible consequences of the war, and many supported the harsh cries that were being raised after the Armistice that the Germans should be made to pay for their 'crimes'. The war-time propaganda had stressed the cruelty and atrocities of the Germans in Belgium and elsewhere, and it had quite convinced the British public that it had been German aggression that had been responsible for bringing about the War itself. The election of 1918 was thus fought in a somewhat feverish, revenge-seeking atmosphere when cries of 'Hang the Kaiser!' and 'Make Germany Pay!' were widespread and won large popular support. Sir Eric Geddes, a Government Minister, expressed this angry and bitter mood forcefully in his election address:

'If I am returned, Germany is going to pay restitution, reparation and indemnity, and I have personally no doubt we will get everything out of her that you can squeeze out of a lemon and a bit more. I propose that not only all the gold

British Empire had been killed, and over two million wounded, and such colossal casualties meant that every town, village and family throughout the land was affected. Soon war memorials were being erected in every city, town and hamlet, and the huge lists of names told of the loss to the community and of the destruction of a whole generation. But every name represented an individual and a family, and each spoke of a personal tragedy where a husband, father, son, or brother had been lost and had left a gap that could never be filled. Here is how a young, tragic girl expressed her thoughts as she stood among the cheering

Post-War reconstruction

A village war memorial

Germany has got, but all the silver and jewels she has got shall be handed over. All her pictures and libraries and everything of that kind should be sold to the neutral and Allied world, and the proceeds given to paying the indemnity. I would strip Germany as she has stripped Belgium.'

Such attitudes, as we have seen, had some influence on the Peace Treaties and helped to prevent the statesmen at Versailles from establishing a just and lasting peace. Few people in Britain, however, were really too concerned about all the complex details of the Versailles Settlement, and they were much more interested in what was happening in their lives at home. After the Armistice the government had begun tackling the immediate task of reconstruction, with millions of soldiers and sailors being demobilised, and with the war-time ammunitions and other factories being closed down or switched to peace-time production. Civilian and returning servicemen alike now looked forward to the bright new future that had been promised them, and their hopes were encouraged by the new promises that were given by the politicians during the election campaign of December 1918.

Coming home

The Post-War British economy

But all too quickly the bright hopes and expectations of the war generation were dashed as the bitter realities of the post-war world became evident. The struggle had been extremely costly in economic as well as in human terms, and the British economy after the War was in a vulnerable and exposed position. Before 1914 she had had thriving industries in shipbuilding, engineering, steel production, mining etc., but the War had disrupted the whole international economic and fiscal system. Some countries had been forced to turn elsewhere for their goods during the War as British industry concentrated on war production, and now these markets were lost to the British producers. Other countries were so devastated by the War they had not the resources to buy British goods, and again there was a loss of markets. The international financial system had also been undermined, and the lack of confidence in the various currencies inhibited trade. The reparations paid by Germany in goods was also a disturbing factor and tended to eat into British export markets. All in all the British industries of the post-war world found that it was now much more difficult to sell their goods, and this in turn cut down the opportunities for employment in Britain as many firms were forced to limit their production and hence their number of employees.

For some months after the ending of the War such problems were hidden by the appearance of a post-war boom to replace the heavy losses in ships and other capital goods, but all too soon the harsh realities of Britain's new place in the economic scheme of things began to emerge. Thus as the heavy industries of shipbuilding, engineering, steel production and mining experienced a loss of demand, so there was growing unemployment in areas like Central Scotland, South Wales, Tyneside etc., where they had been prominent. Heavy and chronic unemployment persisted throughout the 1920s, and culminated in the Great Slump of the early 1930s. Millions of men in Britain were unemployed in this period, and many of the ex-servicemen among them felt they had been betrayed. Their old optimism vanished in the misery of the dole queues, and their bitterness was increased by the sight all around them of sleek, fat men who had made substantial profits from providing materials for the war effort. The war profiteers, it seemed, had gained all the benefits from the War, while the poor, suffering soldiers had died for a mere pittance in the trenches. Even the government was described as 'a lot of hard-faced men who look as if they had done very well out of the war'.

The general living standards and living conditions in Britain also produced considerable disappointment and disillusionment after 1918. The Government had introduced some measures dealing with education and votes for women in 1918, but there were to be no real advances in providing better welfare and social policies as had been hoped. The Government did introduce some improvements and extensions in the National Insurance provisions, but it also established a means test to ferret out a man's income and possessions before he was given a supplementary benefit or dole. In housing there were substantial improvements as Acts were passed requiring local authorities to build and rent houses, but the number built came nowhere near the required targets. To many forced to continue living in a 'single end' or a 'room and kitchen' the old promise of the politicians to provide 'homes for heroes' must have seemed a grim mockery. Real poverty continued to exist among certain sections of the community, and the sight of disabled soldiers begging on the streets of Britain was a sad and terrible commentary on all the war-time plans and promises.

A new council estate, Glasgow

Post-war pacifists

Attitudes to the War

Such conditions and the general disillusionment which accompanied them helped bring about a significant change in many people's attitude towards the War itself during the 1920s. Men and women looked back on all the horrors of the battlefields and the trenches, and now they began to question if the terrible sacrifices had really been worthwhile. Some turned to pacifism and declared that the evils of war should be rejected for ever by all civilised countries, and indeed there was a new determination that never again should the young men of Britain be called upon to engage in mutual slaughter on the battlefields. Such attitudes were increasingly reinforced as men read over the writings of the war poets whose vivid verse descriptions of the horrors of war shocked and startled the imagination:

'What passing-bells for these who die as cattle?
Only the monstrous anger of the guns.
Only the stuttering rifles' rapid rattle
Can patter out their hasty orisons.
No mockeries for them; no prayers nor bells,
Nor any voice of mourning save the choirs, –
The shrill, demented choirs of wailing shells;
And bugles calling for them from sad shires.'

(Wilfrid Owen; *Anthem for Doomed Youth*)

'I worked in a great shipyard by the Clyde;
There came a sudden word of wars declared,
Of Belgium, peaceful, helpless, unprepared,
Asking our aid: I joined the ranks, and died.
*I gave my life for freedom – This I know
For those who bade me fight had told me so.*'

(W.N. Ewer; *Five Souls*)

'"Good-morning, good-morning!" the General said,
When we met him last week on our way to the line.
Now the soldiers he smiled at are most of 'em dead,

And we're cursing his staff for incompetent
swine.
"He's a cheery old card," grunted Harry to Jack
As they slogged up to Arras with rifle and pack.
But he did for them both by his plan of attack.'

(Siegfried Sassoon; *The General*)

The impact of such verses helped to bring home
to the people of Britain the horror and the futility of
war, and increasingly they began questioning the
whole point and purpose of it all. Books were
published denouncing the politicians who had been
responsible for the outbreak of the war, and
criticising the generals for their conduct of the
fighting. At the same time many young people came
to turn away from the War in a different way by
seeking to forget in a frenzied social life. In London
and other cities there was such an intense concentration on dancing, jazz music, parties and general
jollification that the period came to be known as
'The Gay Twenties', and it seemed almost as if the
young generation wished to blot out completely the
grim memories of the War.

Permanent consequences of the War

And yet despite this apparent attempt on the part of
many people to forget the War and to seek escape
from its memories in many different ways, the first
World War had a deep and permanent effect on
British society. The huge losses, for example, had a
long-lasting impact on the form and structure of the
population of Britain, and everywhere there were
gaps that profoundly affected every aspect of life. In
every town, village, industry, club or institution
there were many absent members and potential
leaders whose work and contribution was sadly
missed, and the many men who might have helped
solve the post-war problems lay dead on countless
battlefields. Men spoke of the Lost Generation, and

it may be that their absence had adverse effects on
business and industry, for no one could possibly
quantify the damage done to the structure and
success of British industry by the loss of so much
talent and skill.

The position of women in British society had
also been radically affected by the War. As we have
seen, the part they had played in the war effort had
won them the vote and a new freedom in work and
in social life. Many found themselves dismissed
from their war-time employment as the armaments
factories closed and as men returned from the
services, but certainly they were playing an increasingly important role in many occupations and
economic activities. It is true that they had still a
long way to go before they achieved real equality in
society, but certainly their role had been quite
transformed from that in pre-war years. This was in
a sense marked by the changes in fashion to a freer
style of dress that enabled women to play a more
positive and active role in the community. This
change in women's fashions was also influenced in a

1920s fashions. Summer

The 'Gay 20s'

rather sad way by the presence of hundreds of thousands of women who had been bereaved and left as widows. Previously it had been customary for widows to adopt a rather formal role and dress, but now the large numbers of young women in this situation made it imperative that they should not be so attired and classified.

1920s fashions. Winter

The First World War had also a very considerable impact on the general cultural and educational life of Britain. There was a new consciousness that the country required a more highly educated workforce, and although the 1918 Act did not provide a full and adequate education for all the country's children, there certainly was an acceptance of the need for vast improvements in the general educational provision. The War, too, had given a considerable boost to science and technology, and the fruits of the war-time research, inventions and developments were utilised to make British industry more efficient and mechanised. In the car industry there was a switch to assembly line production, while the development of the aircraft industry and air travel had been greatly accelerated by the intense struggle to develop new and improved planes for the rival air forces in France. The development of science, together with the general reaction against the horrors of the conflict, had also had a dramatic effect on the place of religion in British society, and certainly there had been a decline of religious worship and observance. It seemed that the frightful realities of modern war had caused many people to question the idea of a benevolent God, and large numbers turned away from such a concept.

The whole pattern of British politics, too, was significantly affected by the War, and it certainly hastened major trends and developments. The War, for example, accelerated the advance of the Labour Party, for several of its leaders were brought into the Government and the centres of political power. After 1918 it became one of the major parties in Britain, and by 1924 it was able, with Liberal support, to form a Government. In the same way the clash between the Asquith Liberals and the Lloyd George supporters in 1916 gravely weakened the Liberal Party, and the post-war years saw a steady decline of this once great party. The

Assembly line workers

control of agriculture. More and more in Britain there was an acceptance of collective ideas and procedures, and the Liberal Party found it difficult to adjust to the new trends in British society. Perhaps it was that the Labour Party with its emphasis on the public or community control of various enterprises was more in accord with these trends, and thus the War by hastening such developments had certainly influenced the structure and content of British politics. The trade unions, linked as they were with the Labour Party, were also affected by the War, for the part played by them and their leaders in the war effort increased the prestige and status of the trade union movement. Trade unions were to advance to positions of very considerable power and influence later in the century, and the War was certainly a significant stage in that advance.

Some critics have also suggested that the class structure and pattern of British society was altered and modified by the First World War. Britain before 1914 was certainly a stratified society with clear divisions between the various classes (see p. 19), and the War did bring about much more contact and understanding between the people of different backgrounds as they met in the services, war work, hospitals or ambulance units. It would be wrong, however, to exaggerate the changes that occurred, for certainly there were still significant class divisions after 1918, although these were now a little muted. There was also a greater degree of social mobility, and thus we might conclude that the shock of the conflict and the urgent needs of the national struggle had done a little to moderate the gaps between people in different walks of life in Britain.

Ireland

In Ireland, as in so many other areas of British life and politics, the War brought about important

needs and demands of the War had undermined its position and played an important part in that revolution which was eventually to see the Labour Party replace the Liberal Party as the main opponent of the Conservatives.

Part of the reason for the decline of the Liberal Party was the tremendous boost given by the War to the idea of the state intervening to organise and control the nation's resources. The old Liberal doctrines had stressed individual rights, individual freedom, and freedom for trade and industry, but the demands of the War had led to the state regulation of industry, to rationing, and to the

Civil War in Ireland. Rebels (left) and the Irish Army (right) fight over the terms of the treaty with Britain

shifts in the pattern and control of Irish affairs. The outbreak of the War had shelved the implementation of the Third Home Rule Bill, and indeed it had helped to dampen down the conflicts that had seemed set to produce civil war in 1914. But some of the Irish Nationalists were still determined to secure independence, and they began plotting to take advantage of the War to advance their cause. Some contacted the German authorities to obtain arms, and then at Easter 1916 a small uprising occurred when groups of armed men seized the Post Office and other buildings in Dublin. This Easter Rebellion, as it was called, was put down by British troops after a sharp struggle, and some of the Irish leaders were arrested and executed. This unwise action turned large sections of Irish opinion against Britain, and the demand for action grew. After the end of the War, there was an outbreak of violence in Ireland, and Britain had to push in soldiers to deal with the armed struggle that she was now facing. The Irish had been encouraged by the policies adopted by the Allies of giving freedom to small countries, and now the United States seemed to be favouring their struggle. At length Britain was forced to agree to a Treaty in 1922 whereby twenty-six counties in the south of Ireland were in effect

granted their independence as the Irish Free State within the Empire (in 1937 the Free State became Eire and a completely independent country). Six counties in the north were granted Home Rule as Northern Ireland, but although it had its own Parliament, Northern Ireland still formed an integral part of the United Kingdom. The War had thus helped to give a decisive push in the long struggle of the Irish people for the right to manage their own affairs.

Position of Britain and Europe

The example of Ireland was to be followed in later years by other people in the British Empire, and in the following decades there were struggles against British rule in Palestine, India and elsewhere. Certainly Britain seemed to be in a uniquely dominant position in the world in 1919 with large new territories gained under mandate and with most of her former rivals thrust out of the picture by the Peace Settlement. But in a very real sense Britain and the other countries of Europe had been gravely weakened in the struggle, and thus, for example, the First World War gave the United States a new eminence and advanced the power of

The rising power. Japanese troops enter Shanghai

Japan in the Pacific. Britain and the other European powers still continued to play a dominant political, economic and military role in world affairs after 1918, but the First World War does mark a significant stage in the decline of Europe that was to become so apparent after the Second World War. In a sense they so weakened themselves by their great internal European struggles and blood-letting that the pre-eminent position they held in 1900 was significantly eroded.

Conclusion

It is clear, therefore, that the story of the First World War is one of the great dramas of our modern world. In those four years between 1914 and 1918 the nations of Europe engaged in one of the greatest struggles in history, and when one examines closely the titanic nature of the conflict, one cannot but be amazed at the sheer endurance and tenacity of the peoples who fought so long and so heroically. The modern observer is quite stun-ned and appalled by the colossal scale of the casualties and losses that were caused through the massed frontal assaults on the trenches, but shining through it all is the sheer, tragic courage and heroism of the ordinary soldiers who endured so much. Rarely can there have been such an epic tale of human courage and heroism, and over the years later generations have looked back in wonder, horror and admiration. Continually the old stories are told in books, novels, films and on television, and each individual and generation seeks to under-stand and make sense of it all. Modern readers can still come near to tears as they see the eager, young faces in their millions marching off to the horror and death of the battlefields, and we can still mourn for the millions of tragedies and the sacrifices that were made. This continuing fascination with the First World War certainly arises out of the sheer drama and intensity of the story, but it also springs from an awareness that it has been of immense importance in shaping our modern world. The people of the time who called it the Great War instinctively recognised its all-embracing signi-ficance, for it was indeed a watershed in the history of Britain and of Europe. We today are still living under its shadow, and in so many ways our lives are affected by trends and forces that had their origin in the great diplomatic and military struggles that made up the First World War.

Before and after (opposite)

Exercises Chapter Twelve

1 a) Describe some of the ways in which the First World War made a permanent impact on British society. *8*

b) Did the War lead to any weakening of the position of Britain and Europe in the world? *6*

c) To what extent was the First World War a watershed in the history of Britain and of Europe? *6*

(20)

2 The first extract is from a book written by Vera Brittain, and the second from a poem written by W.N. Ewer.

'For the first time I realised, with all that full realisation meant, how completely everything that had hitherto made up my life had vanished with Edward and Roland, with Victor and Geoffrey. The war was over; a new age was beginning: but the dead were dead and would never return.'

'I gave my life for freedom – This I know For those who bade me fight had told me so.'

a) Describe and account for the conflicting reactions that affected the people of Britain on Armistice Day. *5*

b) Make some estimate of the losses and sacrifices that the people of Britain had endured to secure victory. *3*

c) In what ways and to what extent had the pre-war Britain vanished? *5*

d) Why did many people in Britain become bitter and disillusioned in the years after the ending of the War? *4*

e) In what ways did people in London and other places seek to forget the horrors of the War in the 1920s? *3*

(20)

3 Imagine you are a soldier in London on Armistice Day in 1918. Describe the scenes you witness and give some account of your feelings as you watch the crowds gathering and celebrating. *(20)*

4 'Was it all worth it?' Imagine you are a disabled ex-serviceman living in Britain in 1930. Write an article under the above title examining the Britain of the post-war world and looking back over the efforts and sacrifices of the war years. *(20)*

Index

Acknowledgements

The publisher would like to thank the following for permission to reproduce photographs:

BBC Hulton Picture Library, pp.6(right), 11(right), 14,18,21(bottom), 26(top and bottom), 27,28(bottom right), 29,31,33(bottom), 34(top), 43(centre and bottom right), 45(right), 58,62,63(top), 64,65(centre), 67(left), 72,76(left), 85(left), 88(bottom), 89,91(top), 95(bottom), 96(right), 99,102(right), 106(top), 107(top and bottom), 111(bottom), 113,114,115,(right), 116,118,120,127,192(bottom), 131(right), 132,133 and 135; Beamish North of England Open Air Museum, pp.102(left) and 129(top); Bettmann Archive, p.4; Bildarchiv Preussischer Kulturbesitz, pp.8,35(top right and bottom) and 43(centre bottom); British Leyland Heritage, p.134; Bulloz, p.6(left); City of Glasgow Department of Architecture, p.131(left); Commonwealth War Graves Commission, p.137(bottom); Mary Evans Picture Library, pp.17,27 and 112; Illustrated London News, pp.21(right), 24 and 119; Imperial War Museum, pp.34(bottom), 45(left), 47,48,49,50,53,54,55,57,63(bottom right), 65(right and left), 66,67(right), 74,75(right), 76(top and bottom), 79(right), 80,81,85(right), 86(left), 87,88(top and centre), 90,91(bottom), 93,94(top), 96(left), 97,98,104,106(bottom), 108,109,110,111(top), 115(left), 121(bottom), 128 and 137(top); Keystone, pp.75(left) and 136; Kodak Museum, p.21(top left); Billie Love; p.86(right); Mander and Mitchenson Collection, p.28(bottom left); Mansell Collection, pp.10,11(left), 20,33(top), 39,63(bottom left), 71 and 121(top); National Gallery of Canada, Ottawa, p.101; Popperfoto, pp.36,84 and 95(top); Press Association, p.28(top); Punch, pp.16,23,40,69 and 100; Roger-Viollet, p.7; Snark International, pp.13 and 46; Society of Friends, p.94(bottom); Süddeutscher Verlag, pp.12,37,43(bottom left) and 61; Syndication International, pp.60,79(left) and 117; Ullstein Bilderdienst, p.35(top left); United States International Communication Agency, p.83; Victoria and Albert Museum, p.21(top centre).

Standing in the way of
control

KASABIAN - EMPIRE